MW01087725

"James Fazio has prod
some dispensationalists will not agree with every point ...
will acknowledge that Matthew 10 and Matthew 28 are two distinct and
different commissions. The commission of Matthew 10 is limited to Israel
with a proclamation of the nearness of the kingdom. In Matthew 28 the
commission is to go to the world with the message of Christ's completed
work on the cross. A very interesting read."

Stanley D. Toussaint, Professor Emeritus,
Dallas Theological Seminary

"In this volume James Fazio wrestles with the puzzling fact that
Matthew's Jesus first tells his disciples not to take his message of the
kingdom to the Gentiles (10:5) and tells the Canaanite woman that, "I was
only sent to the lost sheep" (15:24). Only after his atoning work on the
cross does he command the gospel to go to all nations (28:18–20). Did
Jesus' plans change? Was the kingdom that was offered to Israel different
from that proclaimed by Paul and the apostles in Acts and the Epistles?
What was Jesus offering Israel when he announced the kingdom (if indeed
he already had the cross in mind)? Without necessarily siding with classical
dispensationalism (which claims the kingdom was postponed because of
Israel's rejection), Fazio raises important questions that every responsible
exegete of the Gospels must engage with. This volume challenged me
again to think through these critical issues."

Mark Strauss, Professor of New Testament
Bethel Seminary, San Diego

"Theological dialog between Christians of different traditions is very important. James Fazio, has written a book which helpfully highlights some of the key distinctives of Dispensational and Covenant theology. His work is charitable, and even-handed. As a Reformed Pastor, I commend this book as a gracious and open door to theological discussion!"

Adriel Sanchez, Pastor
North Park Presbyterian Church

"There is a theological fog that rolls in when there is a failure to observe the prominent change that took place part way through Christ's earthly ministry. One of the issues that is affected by this is Christ's commissions to His apostles. James Fazio's book asks important questions and gives reasonable answers to the two commissions given by the Lord. This book will bring clarity to the gospel record as well as the scriptures that follow. Once again, theological ideas must emerge from solid exegesis rather than imposing its will on the biblical text."

Dr. Paul Benware, Author/Speaker

"I wish more books were written in this manner. Whether you agree or disagree with the points James Fazio makes in *Two Commissions* you'll benefit from the biblical exegesis he uses to make them, and you'll grow in an understanding of the Great Commission."

Matt Smith, Pastor
Barabbas Road Church

"*Two Commissions* serves as a commission from author James Fazio, challenging the reader to think through the Gospel of Matthew critically! In the frustrating tug-o-war of various theological camps, this work gives a balanced framework of the Gospel of Matthew. I truly appreciate this book as the author presents the flow and structure of this wonderful gospel in a clear and palatable way. A great read for the serious student of the Bible!"

Gunnar Hanson, Pastor
Valley Baptist Church

"James Fazio's effort is to be commended for depth of scholarship, devotion to literal, contextual interpretation of texts, and respect toward those who have wrestled theologically with matters of continuity and discontinuity between Israel and the Church. Both covenant theologians and dispensationalists will profit from this thorough management of the two commissions of Jesus Christ. Though Matthew's gospel has long been understood as the clearest presentation of dispensational shift from Israel to the Church, the author skillfully weaves commissional content from the other gospels and Acts so that a comprehensive assessment of the questions facing both covenant and dispensational views can be accomplished. Line upon line, precept upon precept..."

Brian Moulton, Professor of Biblical Studies
San Diego Christian College

TWO COMMISSIONS

TWO MISSIONARY MANDATES
IN MATTHEW'S GOSPEL

JAMES I. FAZIO

Southern California Seminary Press
El Cajon, California

TWO COMMISSIONS: Two Missionary Mandates in Matthew's Gospel

©2015 James Fazio

Published by Southern California Seminary Press
El Cajon, CA

ISBN – 978-0-9864442-0-3

Unless otherwise noted, all Scripture quotations are from The Holy Bible, New King James Version (NKJV), copyright © by Thomas Nelson, 1984.

DEDICATION

To the faithful men at Southern California Seminary
whose example in God's Word has influenced me
to study to show myself approved unto God
as a workman who need not be ashamed.

PROLEGOMENA

Before Jesus ever said, "Go into all the world" (Mk 16:14) and "make disciples of all the nations" (Mat 28:19), He first said: "Do not go into the way of the Gentiles, and do not enter a city of the Samaritans. But go rather to the lost sheep of the house of Israel" (Matt 10:5-6).

Matthew's Gospel contains two discernible missionary mandates where Christ sent His disciples to two different people groups with two evidently distinct messages. The command of Jesus to "Go therefore and make disciples of all the nations, baptizing them in the name of the Father and of the Son and of the Holy Spirit" (Matt. 28:19) is well known and oft repeated by Christians the world over. This missionary mandate has come to be commonly referred to as "the Great Commission." However, there remains another commission with which the diligent reader of Scripture must come to terms.

This book carefully considers these two missionary mandates within the context of Matthew's Gospel, with a view to understanding what may otherwise be perceived as two contradictory commissions. Each of these commissions will be considered in detail, with attention on the context in which each message was given, the content of each message, the intended audience, and other distinctive features which serve to distinguish them.

Following an examination of the biblical text, a theological evaluation is offered in an attempt to develop a framework for understanding the Evangelical mandate which most Christians regard as binding upon the Church today.

TABLE OF CONTENTS

iv

TABLES and ILLUSTRATIONS

vi

PREFACE

Similarities and distinctions form the basis for our understanding of the world. It's been said that we live in an Information Age because significant strides have been made in technology and the sciences. What has made this leap forward possible is our development in understanding the natural world through the parsing out of its elements. By recognizing where one thing begins and another ends we are better equipped to understand how all things work together to form a cohesive whole.

Consider for a moment the periodic table of elements with its arrangement of the chemical elements organized on the basis of their atomic numbers, electron configurations, and recurring chemical properties. Each of these are distinguished from each other and yet they are grouped into similar classifications such as solids, liquids, gas, metals, metalloids, and non-metals.

It's been said that the first systemization attempts began in the late 1700s and went through a number of variations over the years that followed until at last, Dmitri Mendeleev was credited with the publication of the periodic table similar to that which is commonly used today. Yet still, discoveries have continued to be made into the twenty-first century. With our increased comprehension of these diverse elements, with each of their component similarities and distinctions, we are continuing to develop a more robust understanding of our material world.

The same can be said of the strides we have made in the medical sciences. Take for instance our increased understanding of neuroscience.

As we have continued to develop our knowledge of the human brain as not merely a single three-pound organ of neural tissue, but as a complex system which can be divided into a six-layered cell-structure called a cerebral cortex, which is distinct from the cerebellum, corpus callosum, and brain stem. The cerebral cortex has been conventionally divided into a right and left hemisphere, each of which consists of frontal, parietal, occipital and temporal lobes. Because of our developed understanding of these distinctions, we are able to perform brain surgery today that rivals the most far-fetched science fiction novels of yester-year.

If we are to make the same kind of advances in the field of biblical and theological studies as we have in the hard sciences, we must be comfortable embracing both the similarities and the distinctions that emerge from the biblical text and to do this without fear that acknowledging these distinctions necessitates the denial of the unified wholeness. To think our text is so fragile so as not to be suitable for the same level of disciplined scrutiny as these other marvelous creations is to deny that Scripture is every bit as much a product of the same Lord and God who formed the natural world in which we live.

A further point can be made from these examples from other disciplines, and that is that difference does not necessitate opposition any more than similarity necessitates identity. Recognizing both similarities and distinctions, where they exist, is necessary to forming a thorough understanding of any part of God's creation. As far as the field of biblical studies is concerned, it can be said that in recent centuries, covenantalists have erred on the side of over-emphasizing the similarities to the exclusion of the distinctions, while conversely, dispensationalists have erred by over-emphasizing the distinctions to the exclusion of the similarities. Moreover, the dominant trend in the Christian church today is that Christians tend to err on the side of an over-emphasis on the similarities, and there are very few voices seeking to draw any attention whatsoever to the distinctions. Therefore, this is one of my chief aims in this book.

As students of Scripture, and moreover as diligent and skilled workmen, we must never shy away from "cutting-straight" the Word of Truth. This term used by the Apostle Paul in his letter to Timothy has been translated "to cut straight" or "to rightly divide" and carries with it the idea of proceeding along a straight path that does not heedlessly intersect with others. We mustn't fall into the trap of false-thinking that says that Scripture requires the reader to turn a blind and forgiving eye to so many contradictions and inconsistencies. Instead, we must embrace the whole council of God, every word (even every jot and tittle, if you will) as it does indeed proceed from the very mouth of God. We must take the two-fold task of letting Scripture speak for itself, and having a ready ear to hear what the Spirit says, all the while, holding fast to that straight course of rightly dividing God's Word of Truth.

x

CHAPTER 1

TWO MISSIONARY MANDATES

"Go therefore and make disciples of all the nations..." (Matt 28:19)

"Do not go into the way of the Gentiles..." (Matt 10:5)

Introduction

There are an estimated 285 million Christians throughout the world today who identify as "Evangelical." One of the primary directives driving Evangelicalism is the apostolic command which Jesus Christ gave His disciples on the Mount of Olives after His resurrection. This missionary mandate, recorded in Matthew 28:19-20, is commonly known as "the Great Commission."

While most Evangelical Christians are familiar with the words: "Go therefore and make disciples of all nations..." they are often astounded to discover that this is only one of two very different commissions Christ gave His disciples within a space of about three years. During His earthly ministry, Jesus assembled the very same band of Jewish followers together and gave them an entirely different apostolic commission: "Do not go into the way of the Gentiles, and do not enter a city of the Samaritans..."

Some might be quick to dismiss this idea, saying that the two are really nothing more than the same commission directed at two different audiences. Others may suggest that the first was simply a prototype of the broader message that Jesus would later ask His disciples to give to the entire world. However, responses such as these risk drawing too hasty a conclusion without giving full consideration to the content of the two messages which Christ gave His disciples to preach on each of those occasions.

Moreover, Jesus directed His disciples to engage in differing actions that were intended to accompany the preaching of these two very distinct messages. The former was to include travelling without any monetary means and shaking the dust off their feet when rejected (Matt 10:9, 14), while the latter was to include water baptism "in the name of the Father and of the Son and of the Holy Spirit" (Matt 28:19).

As uncomfortable as it may be for some to admit, the conclusion is quite certain. Christ gave two different missionary mandates whereby He sent His disciples to two different people groups with two very different messages. This is not intended as a polemical statement, nor is it one that must necessarily result in a particular theological conclusion. It is a mere grammatical and historical observation that arises from studying the biblical text, and one that demands further attention than it has been given by students of the biblical text.

The question necessarily arises, "If the Gospels reveal more than a single missionary mandate, why is it that most Christians have never heard of any other commission besides the Great Commission?" This question is especially poignant given the fact that the Evangelical tradition identifies so strongly with the Great Commission.

If there is more than a single commission contained in the Gospels, Evangelicals should be able to provide rationale for why they keep one and not the other. That is precisely what this book is intended to do. It will offer a thorough investigation of the biblical text surrounding each of these two commissions. Afterwards, it will consider differing theological positions that have emerged among Evangelicals concerning these two missionary mandates. Finally, it will offer an explanation as to how readers should best understand the purpose behind each of these two commissions as well as their impact on Christian readers today.

Christians tend to like the idea of keeping the message of the Bible as simple as possible. Rightfully so. For the sake of ease in communicating the Gospel with others, this is not a bad idea. There is nothing to be gained from over-complicating God's message to man. There may have been a time in Church history when this was the deliberate tactic of some ecclesiastical authorities whose chief concern was to retain power and control over the masses. Nevertheless, this tactic for manipulation has no inherent value for today's reader of the Bible. In fact, the reverse may be said: adding needless complexity to the divine message is detrimental and can only lead to making an otherwise clear message more obtuse and therefore less understandable and/or accessible to the common man.

For the sake of evangelism, there is value in following the "KISS" principle: "Keep It Simple Sweetheart." After all, it would present unnecessary challenges to try to share the entire message of God to man, as it is expressed across sixty-six different books, written by nearly forty different authors in three different languages over a period of over 1,500 years. Developing an ever-increasing understanding of the whole counsel of God is a life-long pursuit.

It is admittedly not necessary for a person to become an expert on every point of theology before receiving the Gospel unto salvation. That point, however, should in no way diminish the need for the Christian to develop a mature and intimate knowledge of the message God has expressed to man throughout all of Scripture. In keeping with the charge of the Apostle Paul, Christians are encouraged to: "Be diligent to present yourself approved to God, a worker who does not need to be ashamed, rightly dividing the word of truth" (2 Tim 2:15).

The kind of diligence which this Scripture refers to is not realized by merely taking those parts of Scripture that appeal to the reader. Nor is it sufficient to consider only those Scriptures which may be effortlessly understood. Neither is it appropriate to gloss over passages that don't seem to neatly fit the pre-conceived narrative to which the reader has already committed himself. Rather, this requires the diligence of a skilled workman or laborer, such as "those who as teachers labor to propagate and promote Christianity among men"[1]

Throughout this book, the reader will be encouraged to exercise this kind of diligence as a skilled worker. The information provided herein is not intended to draw conclusions but to raise important questions—and particularly, to bring to the surface some of the types of issues which readers may otherwise be quick to dismiss. It may well be that some readers are entirely unfamiliar with the two commissions that are discussed in this book, while others may have deliberately chosen to ignore or otherwise minimize the contrast between the two. The approach here will be to bring that contrast to the surface and address it head on.

---

[1] Joseph H. Thayer, *Thayer's Greek-English Lexicon of the New Testament* (1896; repr. Peabody, MS: Hendrickson Publishers, 2000), 248.

Continuity and Discontinuity

Students of Scripture, and particularly those who have some background in theological studies, may be acquainted with the issue of continuity and discontinuity as it relates to the two testaments which comprise the biblical text. Simply stated, the question has to do with how much continuity, or lack thereof, exists between the Old and New Testaments. The late biblical expositor, Dr. S. Lewis Johnson, made famous this discussion, in his "The Divine Purpose" teaching series.[2] Sometime afterward, a book titled *Continuity and Discontinuity: Perspectives on the Relationship Between the Old and New Testaments* was published in honor of his contribution to this topic.[3]

Framed in other theological jargons, a similar question emerges in the discussion of the systems of theology known as "Covenant" and "Dispensational." Within this context, the debate typically centers around the identity of the elect people of God as they are expressed throughout the Old and New Testaments, namely Israel and the church: "Is the church a seamless continuation of the same community of believers from the Old Testament, or is it an altogether new creation, that is neither Jew nor Gentile?"

At the risk of oversimplifying, it may be said that the traditional position of the Covenantalist might appear something like this: The apostolic ministry of the disciples of Christ is a mere continuation of what

---

[2] SLJ Institute, "The Divine Purpose," The Believers Chapel Dallas, accessed February 6, 2015, http://sljinstitute.net/category/the-divine-purpose/.

[3] John S. Feinberg, *Continuity and Discontinuity: Perspectives on the Relationship Between the Old and New Testaments* (Wheaton, IL: Crossway Books, 1988).

Christ had been doing throughout His entire earthly ministry; moreover, is it an extension of that same missionary work which God had performed through the nation of Israel in the Old Testament, beginning as far back as the call of Abraham (Gen 12:1-3), or even from the expulsion of Adam from the Garden.

Conversely, the traditional position which uniquely characterizes the dispensational view may appear thusly: The apostolic ministry recorded in the Acts of the Apostles is indicative of a new work which God initiated in Jerusalem on the Day of Pentecost with the descent of His Holy Spirit (Acts 2).

It should be noted that the terms continuity and discontinuity are not synonymous with covenant and dispensational theology. Rather, certain themes tend to emerge when dealing with these kinds of questions that are generally treated one of two ways. Either one acknowledges the tension that exists in certain contexts, such as between the Old and New Testaments, or the identity of Israel and the Church, or else one tends to sweep over them with a broad brush. At the risk of over-simplifying the issue, it may be said that those who align themselves with the former tradition (Covenantalism) typically fall in step with the continuity view, while those who identify with the latter (Dispensationalism) find themselves favoring the discontinuity view.

Despite the enduring nature of this debate, Christians tend to find general agreement in the notion that there is, at least to some extent, both continuity and discontinuity between the two testaments. At a minimum, continuity exists to the degree that the love and grace of God demonstrated toward man has remained a constant theme throughout the body of Scripture. This theme emerges as early as the third chapter of Genesis, when God restrained His hand in those early days in the Garden of Eden when man showed no restraint, but stretched forth his hand in defiance of God's prohibition to abstain from the fruit of the tree of knowledge of good and evil.

Whereas man's blood would have been the just penalty for this offense, instead the blood of "the Lamb slain from the foundation of the world" (Rev 13:8) was applied, having been prefigured in the flesh of animals which God provided as a covering for their sin (Gen 3:21). For centuries that followed, the blood of animals was spilled on altars as an offering for sin, even though "it is not possible that the blood of bulls and goats could take away sins" (Heb 10:4), until at last, the true spotless Lamb was lifted-up on a cross, having been "foreordained before the foundation of the world" (1 Pet 1:20) for that very purpose. These elements serve well to demonstrate the continuity between the Testaments.

Conversely, Christians do not deny that the New Testament provides a rule for living that would be altogether foreign to the people of Israel such as is depicted throughout the Old Testament. The recurring theme throughout the pages of the New Testament is that Christians are no longer bound to keep the whole Mosaic Law: "you are not under the law but under grace" (Rom 6:14). With that rule comes a new mode of worship. Christians are no longer bound to travel to the temple in Jerusalem bearing animal sacrifices. This is in keeping with Jesus' prediction that "the hour is coming, and now is, when the true worshipers will worship the Father in spirit and in truth" (Jn 4:23).

Elsewhere, the author of Hebrews expressly declares that "God, who at various times and in various ways spoke in time past to the fathers by the prophets, has in these last days spoken to us by His Son" (Heb 1:1-2). The meaning of this text is unmistakable. God at one time spoke in one way, but now He has spoken in a different way. This does not mark a change in the Person of God, but rather in the way which He operates.

The conclusion that many Christians generally reach is that there is both continuity and discontinuity between the Old and New Testaments. God has continued what He started at the beginning, though He has proceeded along what at times may appear from the perspective of man to be seemingly discordant lines. Nevertheless, God is immutable: with Him "there is no variation or shadow or turning" (Jas 1:17).

Seldom is the discussion of continuity or discontinuity applied to the Gospels—which serve in a manner of speaking, as the bridge between the Old and New Testaments. If it is understood that discontinuity exists between the Old and New Testaments, at what point does it occur? It is generally understood that this transition is rooted at Calvary, being signified by the rending of the veil in the temple (Matt 27:51).

If such a notable transition did occur, then one would be justified in expecting that Jesus' post-ascension ministry should bear certain distinguishable characteristics from His earthly ministry. This does not mean that they must be regarded as entirely discordant, but that there should be notable differences.

While two very different views have been offered by theologians on opposite ends of the covenantal/dispensational spectrum, surprisingly, adherents from both camps have agreed on the point that the Great Commission in Matthew 28:19-20 is a seamless continuation of Jesus' earthly ministry. This point will be elaborated on in chapter five. It is essential, however, to first thoroughly consider the biblical text prior to evaluating the conclusions which define these different theological camps. Suffice it to say, this book will take exception to each of these positions.

This study will present an altogether different perspective concerning the Great Commission than those offered by adherents of covenantalism and dispensationalism. This is not to say that novelty is the chief aim of this book, for it is not. Neither is it the goal of this study to affirm (or deny) the positions of any particular theological camp. Rather it is to present a diligent and consistent exegetical approach to the Scriptures and to reveal those themes which are drawn directly from the text. Only after this necessary first set will theological implications emerge as a capstone to this study.

It is important for the student of Scripture to note that theological queries are not typically so easily answered when framed in an either/or question. Such bifurcation often results in the logical fallacy commonly known as a "false dilemma," where the observer may be forced to choose between the less unlikely of two options. The failure of this approach may be demonstrated in any number of ways; however, here are a few related specifically to biblical issues: "Is Jesus God or is He man?" "Is the Bible a human book or is it divine?" "Are men chosen by God or do they choose to believe?" Questions like these represent false dilemmas, and the student of Scripture would do well to avoid them.

A more fitting way to frame such questions might be: "What does the Bible reveal concerning the nature of Jesus Christ?" "What manner of presentation does the Scripture make concerning itself with regard to its origin?" "Concerning the issue of man's salvation, to whom does Scripture ascribe agency?" Such questions direct the inquirer to study Scripture in order to discover what matter of testimony God has given concerning these issues, rather than appealing merely to the limited faculties of human reasoning. It may well be that either question could direct the student of Scripture to the same conclusion, but there is much to be said for how one frames the question.

In the case of the continuity and/or discontinuity presented in Matthew's Gospel, both themes will emerge throughout the course of this work. Neither of these concepts should be seen to necessarily argue for the exclusion of the other. Moreover, no deliberate attempt will be made by the author to stifle or suppress any explicit or implicit themes that arise from the biblical text. All discussion concerning the theological implications derived from those concepts will be treated in chapter five, only after the biblical text has been duly considered.

Delineation of the Study

Matthew's Gospel contains two discernible missionary mandates where Christ sent His disciples to two different people groups with two evidently distinct messages. This book will focus on the observable distinctions between these two commissions as they are attested to throughout Matthew's Gospel and corroborated by analogous witnesses, such as Luke and the other writers of the New Testament. While this study is primarily centered on the witness of Matthew, comparisons will be drawn against select passages throughout the Old and New Testaments for purposes of clarity and definition.

An historical-grammatical interpretive methodology will be consistently applied to the entire Gospel of Matthew, in survey fashion, beginning with the genealogy contained in the prologue, and culminating in Christ's sending out of His disciples to all nations. This missionary mandate commonly referred to as "the Great Commission" will be weighed against the earlier ministry of Christ—paralleling that of John the Baptist—which had the singular theme: "Repent, for the kingdom of heaven is at hand," along with the corresponding apostolic imperative to promote that particular message—referred to throughout this work as "the Germinal Commission."

The term "Germinal Commission" is not a technical term, nor is it one that should be familiar to most readers. Rather, this term has been chosen by the author to distinguish the original missionary mandate which Christ gave His disciples during His earthly ministry (Matt 10; Mark 6:7-13; Lk 9:1-6; 10:1-16), which He restricted His disciples to take only to "the lost sheep of the house of Israel" (Matt. 10:6). The term "germinal" has been selected by the author because it connotes an introductory or seed form of a message that would sometime afterward take root and come to fruition.

These two different commissions will be the subject of the following two chapters. Chapter two will consider the former commission, while chapter three will consider the latter. Each of these chapters will follow a similar format: one which appears to have been deliberately intended by the Gospel writer himself. This format, which emerges when reading through the Gospel of Matthew, is expressed in the following way: context, content, compliment, commission, and consequent (i.e. that which accompanies the carrying-out of the commission).

Chapter two will survey the contents of Matthew 1-10 with attention given to the character of Christ's preaching throughout His earthly ministry. Chapter three will survey the contents of Matthew 16-28, with emphasis on the directive Christ gave to the apostles after His ascension. This will set the stage for the juxtaposition of Christ's earthly ministry and His post-ascension ministry.

Chapter four will provide analogous support to Matthew's Gospel, offering much needed context for the reader to understand how the apostles received and acted upon the command of Christ given to them in Galilee. Primary consideration will be given to Luke's testimony, including both his Gospel account and the Acts of the Apostles. Additional support will be provided through the testimony of Paul.

Chapter five will consider the resulting theological implications which emerge from this look at the harmony and dissonance of the two commissions presented in Matthew's Gospel. Included in this chapter will be an analysis of common views espoused by Bible expositors from both the covenantal and dispensational perspectives. Both positions will be evaluated and the issue of continuity and discontinuity will once more be addressed.

Chapter six will offer a summary of the discussion building off of the exegetical observations of the text. In this concluding chapter, the resultant theological implications of the harmony and dissonance of the two commissions will be duly weighed. Because of the historical-grammatical interpretive methodology that will be consistently employed throughout this study, dispensational distinctions will emerge as requisite to reconciling the distinctions between the two commissions, as well as for developing a holistic understanding of the overall purpose of Matthew's Gospel.

Throughout this book, the context, content, compliment, and consequent of these two commissions will be carefully contrasted and compared against one another in light of the backdrop of Matthew's Gospel. Consideration will be given to the intended recipients to whom Jesus directed His disciples, the thrust of the two messages, and the several complementary and contradictory components which are germane to each of the commissions. Each chapter concludes with a table that is intended to illustrate the concepts that are described therein, as a summary of the main points.

Commission	Mandate	Ministry	Context
The Germinal Commission (Matt 10:5-7)	"Do not go the way of the Gentiles..." (Matt 10:5)	Earthly (Matt 4:17-27:50)	Matthew 1-10
The Great Commission (Matt 28:18-20)	"Go therefore and make disciples of all the nations..." (Matt 28:19)	Post-ascension (Matt 28ff)	Matthew 16-28

Commission Context – Table 1.1

CHAPTER 2
THE GERMINAL COMMISSION

And when He had called His twelve disciples to Him, He gave
them power over unclean spirits, to cast them out, and to heal all
kinds of sickness and all kinds of disease.... These twelve Jesus sent
out and commanded them, saying: "Do not go into the way of the
Gentiles, and do not enter a city of the Samaritans. But go rather
to the lost sheep of the house of Israel. And as you go, preach,
saying, 'The kingdom of heaven is at hand.' Heal the sick, cleanse
the lepers, raise the dead, cast out demons. Freely you have
received, freely give." (Matt 10:1; 5-8)

Context

Christ's mandate that His disciples should preach "the kingdom
of heaven is at hand" appears only in the Gospel of Matthew. This does
not come as a surprise, as only Matthew's Gospel offers as its central
theme the coming of the Jewish Messiah, the Heir of David and Seed of
Abraham. While other Gospel writers were no less concerned with the
ministry of Christ, Matthew's chief purpose was to highlight Jesus as the
long awaited King of the Jews. This point is made evident as early as the
opening declaration of this Gospel narrative: "The book of the genealogy
of Jesus Christ, the Son of David, the Son of Abraham" (Matt 1:1).

Beginning with these words, Matthew proceeds to illustrate for the reader how Jesus Christ should be chiefly considered as the fulfillment of the prophetic covenants which God had previously made with Abraham (Gen. 17:4-8) and David (2 Sam 7:12-16). Unlike what is evidenced by the genealogy recorded in Luke, Matthew's chief concern is not to highlight Jesus' humanity as a "son of Adam" (Luke 3:38). Neither like John, is it Matthew's primary aim to reveal Jesus' divinity as the "Son of God" (John 1:49; 10:36; 11:4; 19:7; 20:31), by tracing His lineage to "the beginning...with God" (John 1:1). Much rather, the clear intent of Matthew's Gospel is to reveal Jesus as the "Son of David" and rightful heir to the Messianic kingdom on earth.

Commenting on the uniqueness of Matthew's presentation of Jesus, Alva J. McClain observes:

> The very first word about Him recorded in the first of the four Gospels deals with His descent from the royal line in Israel; and thus the written record is named "The book of the generation of Jesus Christ, the son of David, the son of Abraham" (Matt. 1:1). To emphasize His royal character, Matthew reverses the historical sequence, putting David before Abraham.[4]

Matthew proceeds to develop the context of Jesus' arrival by demonstrating to the reader that "Jesus was born in Bethlehem of Judea in the days of Herod the king" (Matt 2:1), thereby indicating the threat that Jesus posed to the one during whose earthly reign Jesus had come. In his subsequent statement Matthew reveals that at Christ's birth He was sought for by Gentile wise men who inquired after Him, "Where is He who has been born King of the Jews? For we have seen His star in the East and

---

[4] Alva J. McClain, *The Greatness of the Kingdom: An Inductive Study of the Kingdom of God* (1959; repr. Winona Lake, IN: BMH Books, 1992), 268.

have come to worship Him" (Matt 2:2). Following this, Matthew offers the prophecy foretold by Micah which declares:

> "But you, Bethlehem, in the land of Judah,
> Are not the least among the rulers of Judah;
> For out of you shall come a Ruler
> Who will shepherd My people Israel." (Matt 2:6; cf. Mic 5:2)

After sufficiently demonstrating how Christ fulfills the Messianic expectations of the Hebrew prophets—not merely Micah's, but Hosea's (Matt 2:15; cf. Hos 11:1), Jeremiah's (Matt 2:18; cf. Jer 31:15), and others (Matt 2:23)—the Gospel writer proceeds directly to introduce the one appointed to herald the coming of the promised Heir. Furthermore, he relates how the herald, himself, fulfilled Old Testament prophetic expectations.

> In those days John the Baptist came preaching in the wilderness of Judea, and saying, "Repent, for the kingdom of heaven is at hand!" For this is he who was spoken of by the prophet Isaiah, saying:
>
> "The voice of one crying in the wilderness:
> 'Prepare the way of the Lord;
> Make His paths straight." (Matt 3:1-3)

Matthew's testimony concerning John the Baptist begins with a definitive indicator, which reveals the time at which the heralding of Jesus commenced: "In those days John the Baptist came preaching" (Matt 3:1). The Gospel writer follows this pattern throughout his testimony. In this way he provides the reader key temporal markers that serve to aid one's understanding of the preparatory nature of the role in which John the Baptist served. Later Matthew proceeds to define this role by quoting

Jesus' reference to the Old Testament prophet: "For this is he of whom it is written: 'Behold, I send My messenger before Your face, who will prepare Your way before You'...If you are willing to receive it, he [John] is Elijah who has come" (Matt 11:10, 14).

Thus, the coming of John the Baptist, and his message of repentance in view of the coming kingdom, serves as the distinguishable backdrop of Christ's earthly ministry and provides context for that which follows. The subsequent chapter then offers the reader a discernible conclusion to the context or setting leading up to Jesus' ministry. Therein is depicted the temptation of Jesus in the wilderness which preceded His earthly ministry (Matt 4:1-11).

At last, after recounting the forty days which Jesus spent in the wilderness, Matthew paints a few final strokes which develop the backdrop for Jesus' earthly ministry by quoting yet another Old Testament prophet—this time, Isaiah (Matt 4:15-16). Subsequent to this, the Gospel writer provides another definitive temporal marker to the reader: "From that time Jesus began to preach and to say, 'Repent, for the kingdom of heaven is at hand'" (Matt 4:17).

From what time? That question is plainly answered in the verses which precede it: "Now when Jesus had heard that John had been put in prison, He departed to Galilee" (Matt 4:12). Jesus' earthly ministry began with the imprisonment of John the Baptist. This is in keeping with his stated anticipation: "He must increase, but I *must* decrease" (Jn 3:30). This, marks the beginning of what has been termed by scholars as "the ministry of the Christ in Galilee."[5]

---

[5] Robert L. Thomas and Stanley N. Gundry, A *Harmony of the Gospels, with Explanations and Essays* (1978; repr. Chicago, IL: Moody Press, 1981), 47.

Two important points are made evident by the Apostle's presentation of these events concerning the Lord's earthly ministry in Galilee: (1) it coincided with the termination of John the Baptist's ministry; and (2) its content is identified with the same words as those which the forerunner had preached: "Repent, for the kingdom of heaven is at hand" (Matt 3:2; cf. 4:17).

In speaking to the first point, McClain offers the following:

> The occasion for the commencement of the ministry of the Messiah is the imprisonment of His forerunner, John the Baptist. The close time relationship is indicated by the word "now" ($\delta\acute{\varepsilon}$) plus the aorist participle "when He heard" in 4:12. The phrase "from then" ($\dot{\alpha}\pi\acute{o}\ \tau\acute{o}\tau\varepsilon$) of verse seventeen further affirms this. Matthew is careful to record his narrative so that it leaves his reader with the impression that John's imprisonment is the occasion for the commencement of the King's ministry. In royal protocol the King does not make His appearance in public until the forerunner has finished his work. Matthew, emphasizing the official and regal character of Jesus follows this procedure exactly.[6]

If Matthew's pronouncement that Jesus is the "Son of David," at the opening of this Gospel, serves as a capstone to indicate the context of Jesus' earthly ministry, then the death of John the Baptist is the event which serves as the end-cap. Thus, the fore-runner's ministry which served, in a manner of speaking, as a royal proclamation preparing the way for the promised Seed of David serves as the context or backdrop to that which is to follow. What remains, then, is a proper determination of the second point listed above, which is to identify the content of the message which Jesus preached.

---

[6] McClain, 268.

Content

The express statement, "From that time Jesus began to preach and to say, 'Repent, for the kingdom of heaven is at hand'" (Matt 4:17) at once serves as a conclusion to all that came before it and an introduction to all that follows. In these words of Matthew the reader is confronted with the proposition that although Jesus had lived for nearly 30 years (Luke 3:23), it was not until this point in His life that He began to preach the particular message that defined His earthly ministry—and incidentally, that of John the Baptist before Him.

Concerning the significance of this transition, Grant R. Osborne comments:

> "From that time" (ἀπὸ τότε) is a significant transition found three times in this gospel (4:17; 16:21; 26:16) and indicates a new start. Several believe that "from that time Jesus began to" (4:17; 16:21) indicates the major sections of Matthew's gospel and divide the book accordingly (1:1 - 4:16; 4:17 - 16:20; 16:21 - 28:20)...More likely, it indicates a new phase to Jesus' ministry. The time of preparation is over, and Jesus begins to proclaim his kingdom message.[7]

This message, so succinctly summed up by Matthew, consisted of seven simple words in the original Greek: Μετανοεῖτε ἤγγικεν γὰρ ἡ βασιλεία τῶν οὐρανῶν. Despite its brevity, a number of grammatical observations can be made from this statement. First, it consists of an imperative: Μετανοεῖτε, "Repent," followed by an explanatory basis for that imperative: ἤγγικεν γὰρ ἡ βασιλεία τῶν οὐρανῶν, "for the kingdom of

---

[7] Grant R. Osborne, *Matthew*, Exegetical Commentary on the New Testament 1, ed. Clinton E. Arnold (Grand Rapids, MI: Zondervan, 2010), 143.

heaven is at hand." Second, the imperative is in the present tense, which distinguishes it from the charge that Peter would later give when preaching at Pentecost (Acts 2:38). Concerning this difference, exegetical commentator Spiros Zodhiates notes:

> When Peter preached his Pentecostal address (Acts 2:38), he did not use the verb "repent" (*metanoeíte*) in the present imperative but in the aorist imperative (*metanoésate*), thus urging his hearers to repent initially. This was to be externally evidenced by water baptism that was to occur only once subsequent to repentance and faith, as indicated by the verb *baptisthétō*, the aorist passive imperative of *baptizō* (907), to baptize.[8]

The present tense of the verb, as used by John the Baptist and Jesus, argues that theirs was not just a call for initial repentance, but the kind of call which was ongoing (perhaps one that might even endure beyond the cross?). Suffice it to say, the preaching of John and Jesus was one which demanded active repentance on the part of the hearers. Moreover, both men offered reasonable validation for their otherwise radical plea: "for the kingdom of heaven is at hand."

The specific identity of this kingdom has been debated by expositors and theologians down through the centuries. While it goes beyond the intent of this study to bring a definitive resolution to this age-old controversy, there are nevertheless certain implications which can be derived from this grammatical expression which are worthy of consideration.

First, this explanation was given as the basis for the repentance which John and Jesus demanded from their audience. The relative

---

[8] Spiros Zodhiates, *Exegetical Commentary on Matthew* (Chatanooga, TN: AMG Publishers, 2006), 17.

nearness of "the kingdom of heaven" formed the foundation for their argument. In other words, the repentance of the Jewish people was not predicated by anything else other than their proximity (whether spatial or temporal) to "the kingdom of heaven."

As expressed earlier, this imperative of John and Jesus contrasts with the one which Peter presented on the Day of Pentecost. There he offers an altogether different basis for repentance: "Repent, and let every one of you be baptized in the name of Jesus Christ for the remission of sins; and you shall receive the gift of the Holy Spirit. For the promise is to you and to your children, and to all who are afar off, as many as the Lord our God will call" (Acts 2:38-39). The basis for Peter's cry for repentance was a promise—namely "the promise of the Holy Spirit" (Acts 2:33) which he had previously identified by name for his audience. Conversely, the repentance sought after by John and Jesus is predicated on the proximity of "the kingdom of heaven" in relation to the hearer.

Second, it can be determined from the Greek tense of ἤγγικεν, "at hand," that "the kingdom of heaven" was neither drawing close, nor was it something to arrive in the near future. Much rather, the perfect tense of the verb reveals that the "the kingdom of heaven" had already drawn near. Concerning this Greek tense, which has been rightly called "the most important, exegetically, of all the Greek tenses,"[9] the following point is made by leading Greek grammarian Daniel B. Wallace:

> The force of the perfect tense is simply that it describes an event that, completed in the past (we are speaking of the perfect

---

[9] James Hope Moulton, *Prolegomena*, vol. 1, *A Grammar of New Testament Greek* (Edinburgh: T. & T. Clark, 1908), 140, accessed February 16, 2013, http://faculty.gordon.edu/hu/bi/ted_hildebrandt/new_testament_greek/text/moulton-grammarntgreek.pdf.

indicative here), has results existing in the present time (i.e., in relation to the time of the speaker). Or, as Zerwick puts it, the perfect tense is used for "indicating not the past action as such but the present 'state of affairs' resulting from the past action."

BDF suggests that the perfect tense "combines in itself, so to speak, the present and the aorist in that it denotes the *continuance of completed action*...."[10]

The grammatical implications stemming from the use of the perfect indicative verb are vast; however, one must also be careful not to commit a fallacy of grammar, as it has elsewhere been noted that "there is no one-to-one connection between the Greek tense form and *time* of the action."[11] Regardless, an argument can be made from the grammar that the presence of "the kingdom of heaven" was regarded by Jesus as something which had already occurred in the past with resulting significance at the time of His preaching. The same can be said of John's message—for the two were identical.

On account of this, Evangelical commentators Edward Hindson and James Borlund conclude: "The message of John the Baptist is now clearly proclaimed by Jesus Christ. However, Jesus as the Messiah, is not calling on His listeners to prepare for the coming of the kingdom but rather announces that the kingdom is here."[12]

---

[10] Daniel B. Wallace, Greek Grammar Beyond the Basics: An Exegetical Syntax of the New Testament (Grand Rapids, MI: Zondervan, 1996), 573.

[11] D. A. Carson, *Exegetical Fallacies*, 2nd ed. (Grand Rapids, MI: Baker Academic, 1996), 73.

[12] Edward Hindson and James Borland, *The Gospel of Matthew: The King is Coming*, Twenty-First Century Biblical Commentary, ed. Mal Couch (Chattanooga, TN: AMG Publishers, 2006), 43.

What sort of determination, then, can be made from this? Both John and Jesus pointed to the arrival of the kingdom of heaven as something which had already arrived with Christ.[13] Grant Osborne clarifies: "In the Messiah the kingdom has arrived, yet the events have only been inaugurated, and the final stage is in the future."[14] This formed the basis for John's and Jesus' call to the Jewish people for repentance.

Thus, both preachers proclaimed that the arrival of the King marked the presence of the kingdom in a manner distinct from that which had previously been known to Israel. While this does not reveal the precise nature of the kingdom, it does help to define it as something more than merely an abstract rule in men's hearts. Alva McClain rightly concludes:

> If the Kingdom, announced as "at hand" by the Lord, had been exclusively a "spiritual kingdom," or as some have defined it, "the rule of God in the heart," such an announcement would have had no special significance whatever to Israel, for such a rule of God had *always* been recognized among the people of God.[15]

The message of John and Jesus was concisely summarized by Matthew: "Repent, for the kingdom of heaven is at hand" (Matt 3:2; 4:17). It could, however, have been very well expanded upon—and indeed it was. In the subsequent chapters, commonly known as "the Sermon on the Mount," that is precisely what Matthew does.

---

[13] Zodhiates, 18.

[14] Osborne, 111.

[15] McClain, 303.

Thus, Jesus' most famous earthly discourse follows in Matthew's narrative just subsequent to the Apostle's claim that "Jesus went about all Galilee, teaching in their synagogues, and preaching the gospel of the kingdom" (Matt 4:23). Commenting on this famous sermon, Osborne remarks: "In Matthew's gospel the Sermon immediately follows the summary of Jesus' kingdom preaching (4:17, 23) and must be seen in that light."[16] This recognition of the content of Jesus' sermon as an exposition of the gospel of the kingdom is essential to developing a proper understanding of the message that He would later commission His disciples to preach (Matt 10:5-8).

What is the content of this sermon? It is the proclamation that the Davidic King has come to fulfill Old Testament prophecy and that the Kingdom which He brings with Him is a rule unlike any they have yet to know. Therefore, His sermon is intended to reveal to the Jewish people the nature and character of that unfamiliar rule—the heavenly standard which far exceeds any earthly rule formerly known to the House of Israel.

This is the content of Jesus' Sermon on the Mount as it is uniquely presented by Matthew. Arno C. Gaebelein explains:

> The Holy Spirit, to carry through the wonderful scope of the first Gospel, has put the words of our Lord together into one continued address to His disciples, in the very midst of the most positive evidences that the King has come and Jehovah is in the midst of His people. When the King is manifest He utters His proclamation. Such is the discourse before us here in Matthew, the proclamation of the Lord Jesus Christ as King. And if the King proclaims, makes known His proclamation, it must be concerning the Kingdom which He came to bring, preached and offered to

---

[16] Osborne, 160.

the people. Let this, then, be the starting-point of our analysis of this discourse. The so-called sermon on the mount is a proclamation concerning the Kingdom, the magna charta of the Kingdom of heavens.[17]

This may well be what motivated expositor Harry A. Ironside to make the following bold assertion: "In the so-called 'Sermon on the Mount' our Lord was not preaching the gospel but He was setting forth the principles of His kingdom...[the reader] must look elsewhere in Scripture for the gospel, which is the dynamic of God unto salvation to all who believe (Rom 1:16)."[18] While that is perhaps too broad a statement, the author's point is none the less taken. To be more precise, Jesus was in fact preaching the gospel, however that gospel differed in content from the one which Peter and the apostles preached at Pentecost and thereafter.

The "gospel of the kingdom" (4:23) which Matthew identified for the reader was no less "good news" for that Jewish audience than is "the gospel of Christ...to salvation for everyone who believes" (Rom 1:16). Though the contrast between Jesus' preaching and that of His disciples after Him is undeniable (and will be the subject of consideration in the fourth chapter of this book), it is adequate for now to simply note that the content of Jesus' sermon as it is expressed by Matthew in chapters five through seven serves as a detailed exposition of Jesus' earthly teaching.

---

[17] A. C. Gaebelein, *The Gospel of Matthew: An Exposition* (New York: Publication Office, Our Hope, 1910), 106.

[18] H. A. Ironside, *Matthew*, An Ironside Expository Commentary (1920; repr. Grand Rapids, MI: Kregel Publications, 2005), 31.

Compliment

Up to this point the context or backdrop of Jesus' earthly ministry has been presented, as has the associated content or message. Both of these harmoniously point toward an earthly ministry of Jesus that was fixed upon "the gospel of the kingdom." The agreement between the context and the content of Jesus' preaching are enough to provide the reader with a framework for understanding the focus and intent of Jesus' ministry as it is presented by the Apostle in the first Gospel.

It is important to realize, however, that Matthew does not then proceed from this step directly to Jesus' commission of His disciples. Rather, he takes deliberate care to order the information so as to supply the reader with complimentary evidence to support the message which he just presented. In other words, Matthew goes from revealing the context, to the content, to the compliment, prior to dealing with the commission. This pattern has been previously understood in the following manner by Stanley D. Toussaint: "In 4:17 the Lord is recorded as preaching; the teaching ministry is presented in 5:3-7:29; then Matthew goes on to show the third aspect of His ministry. His power over disease, demons, and nature (8:1-9:34)...the character of the miracles bears witness to the Messiahship of Jesus and the nearness of the kingdom."[19]

One may argue that the order of these events should be attributed more to the purposefulness of Jesus' doing, rather than to the authorial liberty of Matthew. However, the fact that Matthew's presentation of these elements differs from those of his contemporaries supports the notion

---

[19] Stanley D. Toussaint, *Behold the King: A Study of Matthew* (Grand Rapids, MI: Kregel Publications, 1980), 121.

that Matthew was purposeful in his intentions. Speaking to this categorical organization, Toussaint contends:

> The order is not chronological; therefore Matthew must have had a purpose in choosing the events which he did and placing them in the section which deals with the King's presentation to Israel. It is evident that the miracles are placed here to show that the King authenticated His claims with great Messianic signs...it shows the power of the King as it will be manifested in the kingdom age. This no doubt accounts for the fact that Matthew omits many details which are found in the other gospels. He is concerned only about giving examples of the Lord's power. Whereas Moses used plagues to prove his message, Jesus uses signs of blessings to authenticate His. The reason for this, of course, was to demonstrate His ability to bring the kingdom if Israel would accept it.[20]

Matthew's purposeful approach in presenting Jesus in this manner is not merely something perceived by biblical interpreters who would seek to read more into his Gospel than he put into it. On the contrary, the apostle is deliberate in the arrangement outlined in the content of this verse: "Jesus went about all Galilee, teaching in their synagogues, and preaching the gospel of the kingdom, and healing all kinds of sickness and all kinds of disease among the people" (Matt 4:23). He cites this demonstration of Jesus' sovereign authority as the reason for His fame spreading throughout the region, resulting in multitudes following Him (Matt 4:24-25). In commenting on these verses, George E. Ladd offers the following:

> Matthew now sketches in a few strokes the ministry of Jesus. After the arrest of John the Baptist, described in Matthew 14:3-4, Jesus

---

[20] Toussaint, 122.

went to the city of Capernaum on the Sea of Galilee and entered upon His messianic work. Matthew describes His message (4:17), the call of the first disciples (vv. 18-22) and the character of the ministry (vv. 23-25). The time involved in these last verses is obviously of considerable duration, for Jesus went throughout all Galilee preaching the good news of the Kingdom of God and healing all kinds of sicknesses as a manifestation of the power of the Kingdom of God among men.[21]

Matthew's outline of Jesus' ministry shows that the preaching of the kingdom was accompanied by the healing of the sick, serving as a confirmation or compliment to the message of the Kingdom which He preached among the Jewish people throughout Galilee. Matthew's presentation of his testimony of Jesus in this summary fashion is a foreshadowing of how the events actually unfold in the course of his Gospel. That is to say that Matthew's account proceeds from context (1-4) to content (5-7) to compliment (8-9). John F. Walvoord takes note of this very pattern:

> Following the pronouncement of the principles of the kingdom in chapters 5-7, chapters 8-9 present the supporting mighty works of Jesus as credentials of the Messiah King...the purpose of Matthew in these two chapters is to offer the credentials of the Messiah as predicted in the Old Testament.[22]

Matthew in no way falls short of accomplishing this task. In the two chapters immediately following the Sermon on the Mount, the

---

[21] George Eldon Ladd, "Matthew" in *The Biblical Expositor: The Living Theme of the Great Book,* ed. by Carl F. H. Henry (1960; repr., Grand Rapids, MI: Baker Books, 1994), 3:29.

[22] John F. Walvoord, *Matthew, Thy Kingdom Come: A Commentary on the First Gospel* (Grand Rapids, MI: Kregel Publications, 1974), 63.

Gospel writer provides evidence which confirms Jesus' message by displaying the works which accompanied His words. In chapters eight through nine Jesus is presented as having authority over nature, demons, sin, and even death itself.[23] Such authority exceeds that of any earthly potentate, falling rather under the exclusive domain of the sovereign rule of the King of heaven on earth.

Commission

Chapters one through nine provide the backdrop as Matthew brings his readers to the determinative moment when Jesus calls His disciples unto Himself to send them out with a specific message. What is that message which Jesus commands His disciples to preach? Matthew declares it in no uncertain terms: "The kingdom of heaven is at hand" (Matt 10:7). This should come as no surprise, for this was the very message that they had heard Jesus preach all along. It is the same message which John the Baptist had preached before Him. This is therefore a continuation of the ministry which began with John the Baptist and centered on preparing the hearts of the people of Israel for that kingdom long prophesied by the Old Testament prophets, and now brought near with Christ's coming to the people of Israel.

While this is not the only commission of Jesus to His disciples recorded by Matthew, it is in fact the first. For this reason—and others which will be expanded upon later—this directive could be termed the "Germinal Commission," inasmuch as it presents the germinal or seed form of the gospel which Christ first preached before He was laid into the

---

[23] Walvoord, 63.

earth, and which afterward bore much fruit (John 12:24). In contrast to the later "Great Commission," this message of John and Jesus was one which was scattered into the proverbial wind to find where it might take up root in the hearts of the people of Israel (Mark 4:3-9, 13-20, 26-32; Luke 8:4-8, 11-15; Matt 13:3-9, 18-32).

Matthew identifies the following four activities in recounting the events surrounding this commission: (1) a gathering; (2) an empowering; (3) a briefing; and (4) a dispatching. Each of these steps is clearly identified in chapter ten and will be considered in turn. The motivation for Jesus' commission of the twelve is clearly stated in the last four verses of chapter nine. Therefore, these verses will be considered prior to an examination of the four activities which constitute the Germinal Commission.

As it has been noted, chapters eight and nine demonstrate Christ's authority over disease, sin, nature and the supernatural. After a series of such demonstrations, Matthew records the following:

> Then Jesus went about all the cities and villages, teaching in their synagogues, preaching the gospel of the kingdom, and healing every sickness and every disease among the people. But when He saw the multitudes, He was moved with compassion for them, because they were weary and scattered, like sheep having no shepherd. Then He said to His disciples, "The harvest truly is plentiful, but the laborers are few. Therefore pray the Lord of the harvest to send out laborers into His harvest." (Matt 9:35-38)

The imagery that Jesus gives is that of a field ripe for the harvest with too few laborers to tend it. The significance of this agricultural metaphor has been stated elsewhere: "food must be harvested at a precise time or the opportunity is lost."[24] This text then reveals the omniscient

---

[24] Zodhiates, 114.

and omnipresent God, clothed in humanity, as acutely burdened with the need to reach the many with this timely offer of the Kingdom. Unable to accomplish this task alone, He directs His disciples to pray that the Lord would send out laborers to assist in this effort.

In this context, the tenth chapter of Matthew's Gospel begins with Jesus calling His disciples to Himself (Matt 10:1a). Matthew identifies each of the twelve disciples by name:

> Now the names of the twelve apostles are these: first, Simon, who is called Peter, and Andrew his brother; James the son of Zebedee, and John his brother; Philip and Bartholomew; Thomas and Matthew the tax collector; James the son of Alphaeus, and Lebbaeus, whose surname was Thaddeus; Simon the Canaanite, and Judas Iscariot, who also betrayed Him. These twelve Jesus sent out. (Matt 10:2-4)

These twelve men were commissioned by Jesus to preach a specific gospel—the gospel of the Kingdom—having not only been given the content of what to preach: "As you go, preach, saying, 'the kingdom of heaven is at hand'" (Matt 10:7), but having been empowered to compliment that self-same message through the working of miracles: "And when He had called His twelve disciples to Him, He gave them power over unclean spirits, to cast them out, and to heal all kinds of sickness and all kinds of disease" (Matt 10:1). Toussaint remarks concerning this need: "to authenticate their message of the nearness of the kingdom, the Lord gave them power to perform signs. These miracles were not to be used merely to instill awe, but to show that the kingdom was at hand (Matthew 12:28)."[25]

---

[25] Toussaint, 139.

By listing each disciple by name, Matthew emphasized that each of the twelve was empowered by God with the ability to perform miraculous works in confirmation of their kingdom message, so that a third time he repeats: "These twelve Jesus sent out" (Matt 10:5). After naming each of the twelve disciples, Matthew recorded Jesus' direct charge to them: "As you go, preach, saying, 'The kingdom of heaven is at hand.' Heal the sick, cleanse the lepers, raise the dead, cast out demons. Freely you have received, freely give" (Matt 10:7-8).

It is significant that Judas, whom the Scriptures declare to be "the son of perdition" (Jn 17:12) was also equipped not only to preach the message of the kingdom but to perform the miracles associated with that message. David Thomas comments on this peculiarity:

> The possession of the miraculous was no virtue. Wicked men might have been endowed—were, perhaps, endowed—with miraculous power, and did many "*mighty works*." There was nothing more praiseworthy in a man being able to effect, by a power given to him at the moment, a supernatural deed, than in the little wire for transmitting the electrical element.[26]

The significance of Judas' demonstrative display of supernatural power is wrapped up, once again, in the Sovereign authority of the Messiah and the kingdom message which the apostles were proclaiming. Like John the Baptist before them, the twelve would be acting as mere messengers or heralds—earthly delegates of the heavenly King—sent to pronounce the nearness of the kingdom to Israel. Toussaint describes the implication of this act: "While Jesus displayed great power by His miracles,

---

[26] David Thomas, *Gospel of Matthew: A Homiletical Commentary* (1873; repr. Grand Rapids, MI: Kregel Publications, 1979), 150.

the delegating of miraculous power to others was the clearest indication of the greatness of His person."[27]

The miracles were intended to compliment the message. The message was intended to provoke Israel to repentance. The repentance was to be motivated by the nearness of the kingdom. The nearness of the kingdom was a result of the appearance of the King to the people of Israel.

A common objection to that last assertion might be: "But Jesus appeared to more than just Israel when He came." While this cannot be denied, it was Jesus' own declaration that affirmed the divine intent behind His coming to the earth: "I was not sent except to the lost sheep of the house of Israel" (Matt 15:24). Jesus spoke in answer to the Gentile woman's plea for help, as recorded by Matthew: "Have mercy on me, O Lord, Son of David! My daughter is severely demon-possessed" (Matt 15:22).

In fact, Jesus' first response was to utterly ignore this Gentile woman's pleas (Matt 15:23) until His disciples pressed Him to send her away, at which point He offered the explanation that He was sent only to children of Israel (Matt 15:24). However, the woman's persistent pleading with the Son of David resulted in another verbal response, less indifferent yet no more favorable than the first: "It is not good to take the children's bread and throw it to the little dogs" (Matt 15:26).

This refusal of Jesus to acknowledge the Gentile woman stands out in the Gospels as uncharacteristic and perhaps even contradictory to the perception that many have of the loving, caring, peace-loving Messiah Who just glides around the earth committing benevolent acts toward all who cross His path. However, it may be seen that this denial is entirely in

---

[27] Toussaint, 137.

keeping with Jesus' own statement of intent: "I was not sent except to the lost sheep of the house of Israel" (Matt 15:24).

Likewise, Jesus commissioned His disciples to go only to the lost sheep of the house of Israel. Moreover, He explicitly barred them from taking their message of the kingdom to the Gentiles (Matt 10:5). In recognition of this fact, Ironside remarks:

> In order to understand rightly the calling and mission of the Twelve prior to our Lord's crucifixion, we need to bear in mind that the Lord Jesus Christ was presenting Himself to Israel as their promised King. God was dealing with them as a nation, giving them full opportunity to acknowledge the claims of His Son. The Twelve were chosen as His messengers to the nation as such, and their ministry, like His own, was primarily to "the lost sheep of the house of Israel."[28]

Jesus' commission of the Twelve is an extension of the Messiah's own earthly ministry. They were to preach what He preached, to the same people to whom He was sent, and they were to signify their message with the same works which He performed in their presence. Every indication given by the Gospel writer confirms that the message and the method of the disciples was no different from that of their Master, or of His herald before Him. Carson explains: "The content of the disciples' message was very like that in 3:2; 4:17. 'Repent' is not mentioned but is presupposed. The long awaited kingdom was now near enough to be attested by miracles directed at demonism and malady."[29]

---

[28] Ironside, 76.

[29] D. A. Carson, "Matthew," in *The Expositor's Bible Commentary: With the New International Version*, ed. by Frank E. Gaebelin (Grand Rapids, MI: Zondervan Publishing House, 1984), 8:245.

Consequent

A final step presented by Matthew includes the stated result or consequent of the Germinal Commission. The message concerning the imminence of the kingdom which was preached by John the Baptist, Jesus, and the Twelve, contained a pronounced consequence which was plainly attested to and confirmed in Matthew's Gospel. This attestation appears most clearly in Jesus' Sermon on the Mount, wherein He declared:

> "Not everyone who says to Me, 'Lord, Lord,' shall enter the kingdom of heaven, but he who does the will of My Father in heaven. Many will say to Me in that day, 'Lord, Lord, have we not prophesied in Your name, cast out demons in Your name, and done many wonders in Your name?' And then I will declare to them, 'I never knew you; depart from Me, you who practice lawlessness!'
>
> "Therefore whoever hears these sayings of mine, and does them, I will liken to a wise man who builds his house on a rock: and the rain descended, the floods came, and the winds blew and beat on that house; and it did not fall, for it was founded on the rock.
>
> "But everyone who hears these sayings of Mine, and does not do them, will be like a foolish man who built his house on the sand: and the rain descended, and the floods came, and the winds blew and beat on that house; and it fell. And great was its fall." (Matt 7:21-27)

In these closing words of His renown sermon, Jesus clearly declares a coming judgment, which is likened to a raging tempest which will indiscriminately beat down upon the wise and the foolish alike. Christ reveals here that those who will pass into the kingdom will most assuredly be first subject to tempestuous wrath. The wise, who are characterized as heeding the words of the Lord: "Repent, for the kingdom of heaven is at hand!" will be delivered; however, those who do not heed these words—even those, like Judas, who performed miraculous works—will greatly suffer.

In reflecting on these words of Jesus, D. A. Carson states:

"That day" is the Day of Judgment (cf. Mal 3:17-18; 1 Enoch 45:3; cf. Matt 25:31-36; Luke 10:12; 2 Thess 1:7-10; 2 Tim 1:12; 4:8; Rev 16:14). The false claimants have prophesied in Jesus' name and by that name exorcised demons and performed miracles. There is no reason to judge their claims false; their claims are not false but insufficient.[30]

The message concerning the coming kingdom, which Jesus detailed on the Mount of Olives, clearly identified a consequent of inescapable judgment. Two options were available to the Jewish audience: they could receive the words and repent, or they could continue on their present course.[31] Either course would lead them to the same destination, for the presence of the kingdom was an inescapable fact; in fact, the King had already arrived. This made the impending judgment all the more imminent.

The intended outcome of the preaching was that repentance would produce a change in the heart of the hearers. As a result the repentant Israelites would be delivered through the wrath that would come upon them. The judgment associated with the coming kingdom would serve to reveal the approvedness of some, just as assuredly as it would expose the disapprovedness of others. This message of judgment

---

[30] Carson, "Matthew," 8:193.

[31] Louis A. Barbieri, Jr. "Matthew," in *The Bible Knowledge Commentary: An Exposition of the Scriptures: New Testament*, ed. by John F. Walvoord and Roy B. Zuck (Colorado Spring, CO: Chariot Victor Publishing, 1999), 34.

which Jesus preached paralleled that of John the Baptist when he chastened the Pharisees and Sadducees who had gathered to hear him speak. Matthew records this event as follows:

> But when he saw many of the Pharisees and Sadducees coming to his baptism, he said to them, "Brood of vipers! Who warned you to flee from the wrath to come? Therefore bear fruits worthy of repentance, and do not think to say to yourselves, 'We have Abraham as our father.' For I say to you that God is able to raise up children to Abraham from these stones. And even now the ax is laid to the root of the trees. Therefore every tree which does not bear good fruit is cut down and thrown into the fire. I indeed baptize you with water unto repentance, but He who is coming after me is mightier than I, whose sandals I am not worthy to carry. He will baptize you with the Holy Spirit and fire. His winnowing fan is in His hand, and He will thoroughly clean out His threshing floor, and gather His wheat into the barn; but He will burn up the chaff with unquenchable fire." (Matt 3:7-12)

John's preaching was a pronouncement of the coming of the kingdom. As such, it was also a declaration of impending judgment—for the two are inseparable. His Jewish audience understood that the kingdom could not come apart from the presence of the King, and the presence of the King would of necessity demand the King's righteous judgment. Therefore, the message which Jesus and John both preached had as a consequent the impending judgment associated with the coming of the kingdom. This would have been completely in line with the Messianic expectations laid out by the Old Testament prophets (Is 1:27; 4:4; 5:16; 13:6-19; 42:1; Jer 33:14-16; Dan 7:26-27) and with "the Jewish concept of repentance which was constantly and closely connected with the Messianic age."[32]

John contrasted his own baptism to the coming baptism of the King. Whereas John's baptism caused men to pass through the waters, the judgment of David's Seed would be one where men would be caused to pass through "fire" (Matt 3:11, 12). This judgment, perceived by John as consequent to the message of the kingdom, was not a matter of probability, but of absolute certainty: "His winnowing fan is in His hand, and He will thoroughly clean out His threshing floor, and gather His wheat into the barn; but He will burn up the chaff with unquenchable fire" (Matt 3:12).

The tenses of the Greek verbs help to reveal the timing in which these events were to occur. In essence, John's message could be understood as follows: "Repent"—now (present); "for the kingdom of heaven has drawn near"—in Jesus (perfect); "even now the ax is laid to the root of the trees"—currently (present); He who holds the winnowing fan will purge the threshing floor—imminent (future); He will deliver the wheat to safety and the chaff to the furnace—imminent (future). The sequence of events had already begun, though it had not found its fulfillment in John's lifetime, nor in Jesus' lifetime. For the prophesied Day of Judgment which accompanied Jesus' preaching also pointed to a future fulfillment.

This consequent which is so evident in both John's and Jesus' preaching is similarly discernible in Christ's commissioning of the Twelve:

> "Now whatever city or town you enter, inquire who in it is worthy, and stay there till you go out. And when you go into a household,

---

[32] Toussaint, 69.

greet it. If the household is worthy, let your peace come upon it. But if it is not worthy, let your peace return to you. And whoever will not receive you nor hear your words, when you depart from that house or city, shake off the dust from your feet. Assuredly, I say to you, it will be more tolerable for the land of Sodom and Gomorrah in the day of judgment than for that city!" (Matt 10:11-15)

In Jesus' sending out of His disciples, He draws a direct correlation between Israel's receptivity to the message of the kingdom and the impending Day of Judgment upon Israel's cities, which He likens to Sodom and Gomorrah. Therefore, deliverance through the future judgment served as a consequent to the message of the kingdom which was preached by John the Baptist, Jesus, and the disciples at the giving of the Germinal Commission.

Conclusion

Jesus' earthly ministry paralleled that of John the Baptist. Their message was the same: "Repent, for the kingdom of heaven is at hand" (Matt 3:1; 4:17). This does not deny that John was a forerunner to Jesus, nor does it imply that Jesus did not provide further elaboration on that message—such as is demonstrated in the Sermon on the Mount—as He had opportunity throughout His teaching ministry. However, Matthew was careful to establish that both messengers carried the same message to the same target audience: the children of Israel (Matt 3:1, 5-8; 15:24).

Matthew explained that the miracles which Jesus performed were intended for the purpose of authenticating Jesus as the promised Heir of David and as validation of His kingdom authority upon the earth. This same authority Jesus committed to the Twelve disciples when He commissioned them to carry the message of the kingdom to the House of

Israel (10:1, 5-8). Just as he had preached concerning the presence of the kingdom and displayed its power upon the earth, so He appointed His disciples to do the same. This is the best understanding of the Germinal Commission as depicted in Matthew.

The table below is offered to illustrate how the distinctive features of the Germinal Commission detailed above can be seen to coincide perfectly with Matthew's presentation of the ministries of Jesus and John the Baptist:

Preacher	Content	Audience	Compliment	Consequent
John the Baptist	The Kingdom of Heaven is at hand (Matt 3:1)	House of Israel (Matt 3:1, 5-8)	Baptism of Jesus (Matt 3:11, 14-17)	Impending Judgment (Matt 3:7-12)
Jesus	The Kingdom of Heaven is at hand (Matt 4:17, 23)	House of Israel (Matt 15:24)	Healing the sick, casting out spirits (Matt 4:23-24)	Impending Judgment (Matt 7:13-26)
The Twelve	The Kingdom of Heaven is at hand (Matt 10:7)	House of Israel (Matt 10:5-6)	Healing the sick, casting out spirits (Matt 10:1)	Impending Judgment (Matt 10:11-15)

Germinal Commission – Table 2.1

CHAPTER 3
THE GREAT COMMISSION

Then the eleven disciples went away into Galilee, to the mountain which Jesus had appointed for them... And Jesus came and spoke to them, saying, "All authority has been given to Me in heaven and on earth. Go therefore and make disciples of all the nations, baptizing them in the name of the Father and of the Son and of the Holy Spirit, teaching them to observe all things that I have commanded you; and lo, I am with you always, even to the end of the age." Amen. (Matt 28:16; 18-20)

Context

The Great Commission is largely considered by Evangelicals to be among the greatest statements ever uttered by Jesus.[33] These words, recorded only in Matthew's Gospel, have resonated in pulpits down through the centuries and have inspired countless missionary undertakings. They have provided the kindling for so much evangelistic fervor that has spread like wildfire across the whole inhabited earth. Moreover, these verses have defined the Evangelical movement more than any other in all of Scripture—and with good reason. In these closing words

---

[33] Toussaint, 318.

of Matthew, readers encounter not merely Jesus' declaration to His disciples, but "the divinely appointed privilege and responsibility of the Church until Jesus comes again in glory."[34]

However, the ideas expressed in these verses are undeniably different from those which Jesus preached throughout the course of His ministry. One expositor keenly observes that Jesus' command here to "'Go' stands in rather sharp contrast to 'Go not' of 10:5. Cf. 15:24. It is clear that the particularism of the pre-resurrection period has now definitely made place for universalism."[35]

However, this climactic pronouncement of the triumphant Messiah does not appear alone as if in a vacuum. It is, in fact, well supported by the preceding context which Matthew provides. This context begins at the second Ἀπὸ τότε ἤρξατο ὁ Ἰησοῦς "From that time Jesus began..." (Matt 16:21), the first of which was discussed in the previous chapter as the starting point for Jesus' earthly ministry. Osborne affirms: "'From that time on he began' (ἀπὸ τότε ἤρξατο) also began 4:17 at the start of Jesus' Galilean ministry, so this introductory formula frames the two parts of Matthew's narrative."[36]

What is it that distinguishes this second phase of Jesus' ministry? The answer to that question is clearly given by Matthew: "That He must go to Jerusalem, and suffer many things from the elders and chief priests and scribes, and be killed, and be raised the third day" (Matt 16:21). Four

---

[34] Ladd, 72.

[35] William Hendriksen, *Exposition of the Gospel According to Matthew*, New Testament Commentary 1 (Grand Rapids, MI: Baker Academic, 1981), 999.

[36] Osborne, 634.

points are outlined by Matthew to indicate this new phase of Jesus' ministry—namely that He would: (1) go to Jerusalem; (2) suffer at the hands of the Jewish authorities; (3) be killed; and (4) be raised on the third day. These four events form the backdrop to and provide the context for the Great Commission.

Matthew's Gospel, then, vividly illustrates for the reader two distinct phases of Jesus' teaching ministry, each of which is clearly flagged by the phrase: "From that time Jesus began to teach..." (Matt 4:17; 16:21). Greek expositor Alexander Bruce comments on Matthew's use of this phrase in 16:21 by acknowledging that this "marks pointedly a new departure" in Jesus' teaching.[37] So divergent is this teaching from any that had come before it that upon first hearing it, the bewildered disciple cried out in protest: "Far be it from You, Lord; this shall not happen to You!" (Matt 16:22).

This response from Peter reveals how foreign this new ministry of Jesus was to that which preceded it. Two years of sitting under Jesus' ministry and listening to His teaching—moreover, proclaiming that very same message himself—did nothing to prepare him for this new phase of Jesus' ministry. At last, with not more than one year remaining on earth,[38] Jesus astonishes His own disciples with the revelation that He would go to the cross and die for the sins of many, and be raised again three days later.

Again, in chapter 17, Matthew records Jesus as repeating this hitherto undisclosed phase of His ministry: "Now when they were staying

---

[37]Alexander Balmain Bruce, "The Synoptic Gospels" in *The Expositor's Greek Testament*, ed. by W. Robertson Nicoll, (repr. Grand Rapids, MI: Wm. B. Eerdmans, 1976), 1:226.

[38] Thomas and Gundry, 117.

in Galilee, Jesus said to them, 'The Son of Man is about to be betrayed into the hands of men, and they will kill Him, and the third day He will be raised up.' And they were exceedingly sorrowful" (Matt 17:22-23). This is followed by a third declaration occurring just prior to Jesus' final ascent to Jerusalem:

> Now Jesus, going up to Jerusalem, took the twelve disciples aside on the road and said to them, "Behold, we are going up to Jerusalem, and the Son of Man will be betrayed to the chief priests and to the scribes; and they will condemn Him to death, and deliver Him to the Gentiles to mock and scourge and to crucify. And the third day He will rise again." (Matt 20:12-29)

The remainder of Matthew's Gospel reveals that this is precisely what unfolds: Jesus leads the Twelve into Jerusalem and the events of the Passion Week ensue. The Son of David's triumphal entry into Jerusalem (Matt 21:1-11), followed immediately by his scourging of the temple (Matt 21:12-17), cursing of the fruitless fig tree (Matt 21:18-19), pronouncements of woe upon the Scribes and Pharisees (Matt 23:1-36), lamenting over Jerusalem (Matt 23:27-29), prediction of His eschatological return (Matt 24-25), betrayal and deliverance to Pilate (Matt 26:14-27:14), substitutionary death for the sinner Barabbas (Matt 27:15-26), crucifixion (Matt 27:27-56), burial (Matt 27:57-66), and resurrection three days later (Matt 28:1-10) all serve as the backdrop to this crowning moment where Christ unveils to His disciples His new directive for them. In this way, Matthew has provided his reader the appropriate context for the Great Commission.

Content

It has been previously demonstrated that the content of the Germinal Commission involved the preaching of the kingdom of heaven to the people of Israel, and was complimented by demonstrations of authority over sin and spirits. The message which the disciples preached paralleled that of their Lord, "Repent, for the kingdom of heaven is at hand" (Matt 4:17; Cf. Matt 10:7). In this regard, the Great Commission is no different from the Germinal Commission inasmuch as the content of the disciples' message can be seen as synonymous with the teaching their Lord demonstrated to them in the second and final phase of His earthly ministry.

Consider the points of Jesus' latter teaching—namely, that He would be betrayed to the chief priests and Scribes, condemned to crucifixion, and raised again on the third day (Matt 16:21; 17:22-23; 20:17-19). These are the very same points that Peter iterated in His first sermon at Pentecost:

> "Men of Israel, hear these words: Jesus of Nazareth, a Man attested by God to you by miracles, wonders, and signs which God did through Him in your midst, as you yourselves also know—Him, being delivered by the determined purpose and foreknowledge of God, you have taken, by lawless hands, have crucified, and put to death; whom God raised up, having loosed the pains of death, because it was not possible that He should be held by it." (Acts 2:22-24)

It is in fact these very points which constitute the Good News, as the Church has understood and proclaimed it for two millennia. In contrast to the former message which Jesus and His disciples preached, this one carries every bit as much significance to the Gentile as it does to the Jew. For this reason, Jesus directed His disciples to carry it into "all the nations" (Matt 28:19), and that is precisely what they did.

Luke records that the risen Lord gave a specific directive to His disciples: "But you shall receive power when the Holy Spirit has come upon you; and you shall be witnesses to Me in Jerusalem, and in all Judea and Samaria, and to the end of the earth" (Acts 1:8). Luke then proceeds to chronicle the accomplishment of this task in the aptly named Acts of the Apostles, which relates the spreading of the Gospel beginning at Jerusalem (Acts 1-7), extending to Judea and Samaria (Acts 8-12), and reaching as far as Asia Minor and Europe (Acts 13-20).

What was the content of their message? Eckhard J. Schnabel offers the following answer to that question:

> The life, death, resurrection, and exaltation of Jesus, Lord and Messiah, is the central, the primary, the dominant theme of the followers of Jesus. This is why the church eventually placed four long texts that narrate the life, suffering, death, and resurrection of Jesus at the beginning of the normative list of books to be read and taught in the church.
>
> The material content of the proclamation of the church is Jesus Christ. The good news (*euangelion*) that the Twelve proclaim is the good news of God's revelation and saving action in and through Jesus, the Lord and the Messiah...The formal content of the proclamation of the church is the testimony of the apostles. The Twelve had a unique role; as eyewitnesses of Jesus' life, death, resurrection, and exaltation, they testify to the truth of these foundational events in God's plan of salvation in an authentic and reliable manner.[39]

---

[39] Eckhard J. Schnabel, *Acts*, Exegetical Commentary on the New Testament 5, ed. Clinton E. Arnold (Grand Rapids, MI: Zondervan, 2012), 106-107.

Absent from the above answer is the phrase "teaching of Jesus." While that may strike the reader as offensive to have it put that way, it is no less true. That is to say, the message which Jesus, John the Baptist, and the Twelve had once preached, never found its way into the preaching of the early church. In fact, it was not even repeated by the very same disciples who had been formerly commissioned to preach it during Jesus' earthly ministry. Why is that? Quite simply, the disciples had been given a new commission.

The good news of Jesus' life, death, and resurrection formed the nucleus of the disciples' preaching. The gospel had effectively shifted from: "Go and tell the Jews that the kingdom is at hand" to "Go and tell the world that I have been crucified and have risen again!" The former message was to result in Israel's repentance; the latter message was to result in the salvation for the nations! Indeed, the latter is "greater" than the former, in a manner of speaking.

However, it trivializes the message to suggest that its intended result was simply salvation for the nations; much rather, the stated goal of Jesus was to produce disciples from all the nations.[40] In fact, it can be seen from the original Greek construction that disciple-making is the governing verb, and thus the central command of the Great Commission.[41] Carson observes: "The main emphasis, then, is on the command to 'make disciples,' which in Greek is one word, mathēteusate, normally an intransitive verb, here used transitively."[42] The other verbs "going,"

[40] Osborne, 1080.

[41] John MacArthur, *Matthew 24-28*, MacArthur New Testament Commentary (Chicago, IL: Moody Bible Institute, 1989), 340.

[42] Carson, "*Matthew*," 8:595.

"baptizing," and "teaching" are all circumstantial and carry less force than the driving imperative to "make disciples." This is attested to by the Greek construction as Osborne notes:

> The circumstantial participle "go" (πορευθέντες) followed by the main verb is a common Matthean stylistic trait, and it becomes in effect another imperative, "Go and make disciples." In fact, the two participles that follow ("baptizing" and "teaching") are also circumstantial and are imperatival in force. Still, the main verb "make disciples" dominates, and all are aspects of that central part of the commission.[43]

Therefore, as it is demonstrated in Matthew, and elsewhere in the writings of the disciples, the commission is rightly fulfilled only insomuch as disciples are made from among the nations. This disciple-making process would occur in connection with the content of the disciples' message—namely that Jesus was rejected, crucified, and rose again three days later. Perhaps nowhere in Scripture is this stated more clearly than in the declaration of the Apostle Paul to the Gentile believers in Corinth:

> Moreover, brethren, I declare to you the gospel which I preached to you, which also you received and in which you stand, by which also you are saved, if you hold fast that word which I preached to you—unless you believed in vain.
>
> For I delivered to you first of all that which I also received: that Christ died for our sins according to the Scripture, and that He was buried, and that He rose again the third day according to the Scriptures, and the He was seen by Cephas, then by the twelve. (1 Cor 15:1-5)

---

[43] Osborne, 1080.

The Apostle Paul reveals through these words the specific content of the gospel which He preached to the nations: "that Christ died for our sins according to the Scriptures, and the He was buried, and the He rose again the third day according to the Scriptures" (1 Cor 15:3-4). He clarifies for the reader that this is that very same gospel which he received (1 Cor 15:3), and the gospel by which the Corinthian believers are saved (1 Cor 15:2). This candid admission of the Apostle plainly reveals the content of the message which the disciples were given to preach at the Great Commission.

Compliment

The message of the life, death, crucifixion, burial, and resurrection of Jesus Christ which the disciples were to spread across the entire inhabited world carried with it a very clear compliment: baptism. Osborne remarks on the uniqueness of baptism to this mission which the disciples were to embark upon: "Not only does the post-resurrection Jesus launch the universal mission; he also launches baptism as the primary sacrament of initiation into the Christian faith. Jesus did not baptize (John 3:22, clarified in John 4:1-2) during His ministry."[44]

Baptism stands as the signifying compliment to the message of the gospel of Jesus Christ. Where previously the demonstration of heavenly authority on earth evidenced the presence of the kingdom, baptism would now serve as the signification that the individual has heard, received, and is now standing in the finished work which Jesus accomplished on the cross. "Baptism" uniquely identifies the one being baptized with that into

---

[44] Osborne, 1080-81.

which he is immersed. Spiros Zodhiates observes: "'Baptizing' (from *baptizō* [970]) means primarily an identity that signifies burial with Christ and resurrection with Him into newness of life (Rom 6:4)."[45] This is precisely how the Apostle Paul used the term in addressing Gentile audiences to whom the idea was otherwise foreign:

> Or do you not know that as many of us as were baptized into Christ Jesus were baptized into His death? Therefore we were buried with Him through baptism into death, that just as Christ was raised from the dead by the glory of the Father, even so we also should walk in newness of life. (Rom 6:3-4)

Paul's teaching concerning baptism "denotes dedication to the service of him in whose name we are baptized,"[46] but it also goes beyond that. Baptism at once refers both to that which outwardly occurs as well as to that which is otherwise visibly undetectable. This latter baptism is what the Apostle referred to when He wrote: "For by one Spirit we were all baptized into one body—whether Jews or Greeks, whether slaves or free—and have all been made to drink into one Spirit" (1 Cor 12:13). It is probably what the Apostle had in mind when he penned the words: "There is one body and one Spirit, just as you were called in one hope of your calling; one Lord, one faith, one baptism" (Eph 4:4-5).

The Apostle can rightly refer to baptism as singular even though there is undeniably one immersion into water and another immersion of the believer into Christ. However, this apparent conflict should be no more problematic than the command of the Lord to baptize disciples into

---

[45] Zodhiates, 517.

[46] Albert Barnes, *Barnes' Notes on the New Testament* (repr. Grand Rapids, MI: Kregel Publications 1962), 591.

the name (singular) of "the Father and of the Son and of the Holy Spirit" (Matt 28:19). Ultimately, the confusion is resolved with the understanding that human agents were commanded to carry out the ordinance of water baptism—i.e. that which is seen—whereas the Divine Agent is the One who carries out the work of Spirit Baptism—i.e. that which is unseen (1 Cor 12:13). Therefore, no ambiguity remains on the part of those to whom this ordinance was entrusted. Baptism was plainly understood by the Twelve and by generations of disciples after them as the requisite compliment to the message of the life, death, and resurrection of Jesus Christ that was to be carried to all the nations.

Commission

With an understanding of the context, the content, and the compliment of the message which was committed to the Twelve, attention should now be given to the commission itself. The words of Jesus to His disciples as recorded by Matthew are as follows:

> "All authority has been given to Me in heaven and on earth. Go therefore and make disciples of all the nations, baptizing them in the name of the Father and of the Son and of the Holy Spirit, teaching them to observe all things that I have commanded you; and lo, I am with you always, even to the end of the age" (Matt 28:18-20).

It is important to observe that Matthew concludes his Gospel with this exultant pronouncement of the risen Messiah. These words form the end cap of the narrative which defined itself at the beginning as: "the book of the genealogy of Jesus Christ, the Son of David" (Matt 1:1). It has been argued that the term "the book of the genealogy" as used by Matthew refers specifically to the recorded lineage which he disclosed in the first chapter and not to the entirety of the Gospel.[47] The opening phrase nevertheless serves well to identify his purpose for writing and as a complement to the words on which he ends the Gospel narrative.

Jesus' opening statement is one of triumph; a proclamation of the King of King's claim to all authority in heaven and on earth. The aorist tense of the Greek verb "to give," ἐδόθη, appears here in the indicative mood and therefore speaks to the time of the action as having occurred in the past with reference to the time of speaking.[48] Moreover, the passive voice of the verb points to the divine agency of the Father and speaks to the work which the Apostle Paul describes elsewhere:

> Being found in appearance as a man, He humbled Himself and became obedient to the point of death, even the death of the cross. Therefore God also has highly exalted Him and given Him the name which is above every name, that at the name of Jesus every knee should bow, of those in heaven, and on earth, and of those under the earth, and that every tongue should confess that Jesus Christ is Lord, to the glory of the Father. (Phil 2:6-11)

Christ's authority has already been established throughout this Gospel. What distinguishes this declaration from any other is the totality of that authority. Carson explains: "'All' dominates vv. 18-20 and ties these verses together; all authority, all nations, all things, all the days."[49]

This proclamation of absolute divine sovereignty over heaven and earth is immediately followed by the newly-risen King's first edict: "Go therefore and make disciples of all the nations, baptizing them in the

---

[47] Osborne, 61.

[48] Wallace, 555.

[49] Carson, "Matthew," 8:594.

name of the Father and of the Son and of the Holy Spirit, teaching them to observe all things that I have commended you" (Matt 28:19). As previously discussed, the Great Commission contains only one imperative command in the original Greek: μαθητεύσατε "make disciples." All of the other verbals are participles, including πορευθέντες, often translated "go," which is an aorist passive participle "designated to indicate a circumstantial action that accompanies the main verb."[50] Therefore, a literal translation from the Greek text would read like this: "Having gone, then, disciple all the nations (baptizing them—to the name of the Father, and of the Son, and of the Holy Spirit, teaching them to observe all, whatever I did command you)" (Matt 28:18-20, YLT).

This is not intended to minimize Christ's sending of the disciples; for the imperative force of the governing verb "make disciples" does transfer to the circumstantial participle "go."[51] However, the emphasis must be understood as resting on the action of making disciples. To simply "go-and-preach" or "go-and-baptize" is not enough. The disciples were given the specific task of disciple-making.

Neither was there any ambiguity as to whom they were sent: "make disciples of all nations" (Matt 28:19). Quite unlike the Germinal Commission, this is a universal command. The phrase πάντα τὰ ἔθνη "all the nations" has been understood in two ways: (1) all the Gentiles, and (2) all the nations.[52] Complimentary passages reveal that this mission would include Jerusalem, Judea and Samaria, as well as the Gentile nations (Acts

---

[50] Zodhiates, 516.

[51] Carson, "*Matthew*," 8:595.

[52] Ibid., 596.

1:8). It would, therefore, be a mistake to take this as the Gentile counterpart to the earlier Jewish commission, for that would narrow the scope that the Lord originally intended.

Another argument for the latter meaning can be made from how the apostles carried out this commission. Shortly after receiving this command they travelled to Jerusalem where they waited for the Jewish festival of Pentecost, following the instructions given to them by the risen Savior (Luke 24:49; Acts 1:12-14). Pentecost became the staging ground for the inaugural preaching of the Gospel message concerning Christ's life, death, burial, and resurrection. Three thousand were baptized on that occasion (Acts 2:41) and "continued steadfastly in the apostles' doctrine and fellowship, in the breaking of bread, and in prayers" (Acts 2:42). That is, they were made disciples.

Luke's narrative of the apostles' missionary endeavors in the Acts of the Apostles suggests that the gospel was not likely to have reached the first Gentile for as many as 10 years after the commission was first given.[53] This supports the conclusion that the phrase "all nations" should not be taken as excluding the Jews, but should be understood as inclusive of all the peoples of the earth.[54]

The apostles were commanded to make disciples of peoples from all nations as they proceeded on their way. The Lord Himself modeled this process for them; He taught them about His suffering, crucifixion, burial, and resurrection three days later (Matt 16:21; 17:22-23; 20:17-19).

---

[53] Schnabel, 473.

[54] Thomas L. Constable, "Notes on Matthew," *Expository Notes*, 2013 ed., Sonic Light, 431, accessed February 16, 2013, http://www.soniclight.com/constable /notes/pdf/ matthew.pdf.

The disciples were to follow that pattern, as were all who would receive their message. Jesus broke that process down into two simple steps by way of the Greek participles βαπτίζοντες "baptizing" and διδάσκοντες "teaching." Speaking to this point, Toussaint points out:

> The method which the apostles were to use to disciple the nations is indicated by the two participles of verse nineteen and twenty. The participle "baptizing" (βαπτίζοντες) is a reference to water baptism which is to be a testimony to initial faith in the Messiah...The participle "teaching" (διδάσκοντες) indicates the second phase of making disciples. The apostles were to teach their converts to observe all things whatsoever Christ had commanded them.[55]

This model was followed at Pentecost, as it is written: "Then those who gladly received his [Peter's] word were baptized...and they continued steadfastly in the apostles' doctrine" (Acts 2:41-42). This pattern was repeated throughout Jerusalem during the early ministry of the apostles; so the followers became the host of believers in the risen Christ who came to be known by the term "disciples" (Acts 6:6:1, 2, 7, etc.). The early church would not use that term to identify the Twelve as distinct from the general assembly—since all were called to be disciples. So, the Twelve came to be commonly referred to as "the apostles" (Acts 2:43; 5:12, 29, 40; 6:6; etc.), since they were those who were specifically commissioned by the risen Lord to spread the Word.

In addition to His explicit command, Jesus offered a concluding consolation: "Lo, I am with you always, even to the end of the age" (Matt 28:20). Matthew closes his Gospel with these words, for what higher words can one give as "good news" than the assurance that the reigning

---

[55] Toussaint, 319.

King of Kings will be with His disciples. This may well be what Luke had in mind when recording the Acts of the Apostles and seeing in their actions the works of the Lord Jesus Christ. Homer A. Kent Jr. offers the following statement in support of this:

> In Acts 1:1...this entire account [the crucifixion, ascension, and resurrection] is summarized as what "Jesus began both to do and to teach." The implication is that what follows in this second volume known to us as Acts describes what Jesus Christ *continues* to do since his ascension as the Holy Spirit empowered believers to carry on the purposes of Christ.[56]

The Great Commission, then, stands at once as both the culmination of Jesus' ministry and of Matthew's Gospel. At the same time, it serves every bit as much as the closing of one chapter as the opening of another—previously unforeseen. The disciples could not possibly have perceived what Jesus was about to usher them into. For this reason, after forty days of presenting Himself to them and "speaking of the things pertaining to the kingdom of God" (Acts 1:3), the disciples inquired of Him: "Lord, will You at this time restore the kingdom to Israel?" (Acts 1:6). To which He answered: "It is not for you to know the times or seasons which the Father has put in His own authority. But you shall receive power when the Holy Spirit has come upon you; and you shall be witnesses to Me in Jerusalem, and in all Judea and Samaria, and to the end of the earth" (Acts 1:7-8).

---

[56] Homer A. Kent, Jr., *Jerusalem to Rome: Studies in the Book of Acts* (1972; repr. Grand Rapids, MI: Baker Book House, 2000), 21.

Consequent

Just as there was a stated result subsequent to the preaching of the Germinal Commission, so also is there a clear consequent to the message of the Great Commission. That result of the preaching of the Gospel of Jesus Christ is the abiding presence of the Holy Spirit. This is seen in the declaration of Jesus at the giving of the Great Commission, as well as each occasion where that Commission is carried out in the biblical narrative.

Matthew closes his Gospel with this parting statement from the risen Lord: "Lo, I am with you always, even to the end of the age" (Matt 28:20). Speaking about these words of assurance, Zodhiates observes: "The risen Christ promises to be 'with' (*metá* [3326]) His disciples, as well as being 'in' (*en* [1722]) them in the Person of the Holy Spirit (John 14:17; Col 1:27)."[57] This promise is unique to the Christian, and quite distinct from any promise which the Lord made during His earthly ministry in all of His preaching to Israel.

In sending out the apostles, Jesus didn't charge them to carry out this new work in His absence. Much rather, He assured them of His perpetual presence. For the last year He had repeatedly told them that He would be betrayed, delivered into the hands of men, and killed. Now, in this declaration, He reveals to them that not only has He risen from the grave, but that He will abide with them forever (lit. "for all days" *τὰς ἡμέρας*). Though His presence will not be revealed until the end of the age, it will no less be a reality for those who heed the words of the Gospel message.[58]

---

[57] Zodhiates, 518.

[58] MacArthur, 346-47.

The abiding presence of Jesus Christ, through the effective agency of the Holy Spirit, serves as the consequent to the Great Commission. Carson remarks: "the Gospel ends, not with command, but with the promise of Jesus' comforting presence, which, if not made explicitly conditional on the disciples' obedience to the Great Commission, is at least closely tied to it."[59] For as many as would receive the preaching of the apostles' message, this abiding presence of the risen Lord would be the certain result.

This stands in stark contrast to the previous commission given by Christ, which had as its consequent the deliverance through the coming wrath or judgment upon Israel. Here, the stated result is the perpetual ministry of the Helper, whom Jesus had previously assured His disciples that He would send: "But when the Helper comes, whom I shall send to you from the Father, the Spirit of truth who proceeds from the Father, He will testify of Me. And you also will be witnesses, because you have been with Me from the beginning" (John 15:26-27).

Conclusion

The discourse upon which Matthew's Gospel closes is one in which Jesus commands His followers go forth and make disciples from all the peoples of the earth. This message differed from the one He had previously given to the same group roughly three years earlier. The former was restricted to a select group of people, the latter was unrestricted. The former required the broadcasting of an announcement, the latter required the making of disciples. The former was to be signified by the working of

---

[59] Carson, "Matthew," 8:599.

miracles, the latter was to be signified by the abiding presence of the Sending Agent.

Admittedly, certain characteristics are undeniably similar: both commissions were given by Jesus Christ; both commissions were given to the His hand-picked disciples; and both commissions were to be a continuation of the ministry which Jesus, Himself, first demonstrated. The conclusion that necessarily follows is simply that Jesus Christ preached, demonstrated, and commanded His disciples to fulfill two distinct commissions.

Commission	Content	Audience	Compliment	Consequent
The Germinal Commission (Matt 10:5-7)	The Kingdom of Heaven is at hand (Matt 10:7)	House of Israel (Matt 3:1, 5-8)	Miraculous Demonstrations (Matt 3:11, 14-17)	Escape the Coming Wrath (Matt 3:7, 11-12; 10:11-15)
The Great Commission (Matt 28:18-20)	Life, Death, Burial, Resurrection (Matt 16:21; 17:22-23; 20:17-19; Acts 2:22-24, 38-39; 4:33; 1 Cor 15:1-5)	All Nations (Matt 28:19; Acts 1:8)	Baptism (Matt 28:23-24; Acts 2:38, 41)	Abiding Presence (Matt 28:20; Acts 2:38)

Two Commissions – Table 3.1

CHAPTER 4

ANALAGOUS SUPPORT

And He said to them, "When I sent you without money bag, knapsack, and sandals, did you lack anything?"

So they said, "Nothing."

Then He said to them, "But now, he who has a money bag, let him take it, and likewise a knapsack; and he who has no sword, let him sell his garment and buy one. For I say to you that this which is written must still be accomplished in Me: 'And He was numbered with the transgressors.' For the things concerning Me have an end."

So they said, "Lord, look, here are two swords."

And He said to them, "It is enough." (Luke 22:35-38)

The Witness of Luke

In the previous two chapters, an exegetical understanding of the life and work of Jesus Christ was developed almost exclusively from Matthew's eye-witness testimony. While the first Gospel is sufficient to reveal the earthly message and ministry of Jesus as expressed in the Germinal Commission, its abrupt ending upon the delivery of the Great Commission fails to offer the reader adequate context for how the apostles received and carried out this second Divine charge. The account which Luke provides in the Acts of the Apostles is the only historical narrative in the biblical record that offers a glimpse into what the disciples actually did in the months and years immediately following Christ's resurrection. For this reason, it is not uncommon for readers of the New Testament to seek to understand the biblical narrative by considering Matthew and Acts jointly. Speaking to this tendency, New Testament scholar Darrell L. Bock explains:

> Many Christians consider Matthew and Acts together, because canonically Matthew is the first gospel and Acts includes the history of the apostolic church. But the canonical link is Luke-Acts, not Matthew-Acts, since Luke authored both volumes. So thinking biblically, it is important to keep Luke and Acts together and tell the story of Acts with an eye on Luke.[60]

It is therefore appropriate to at least briefly consider the testimony of Luke's analogous Gospel along with its continuing narrative as it is contained in the Book of Acts.

Luke begins his Gospel with the following statement of purpose:

> Inasmuch as many have taken in hand to set in order a narrative of those things which have been fulfilled among us, just as those who from the beginning were eyewitnesses and ministers of the word delivered them to us, it seemed good to me also, having had perfect understanding of all things from the very first, to write to you an orderly account, most excellent Theophilus, that you may know the certainty of those things in which you were instructed. (Luke 1:1-4)

---

[60] Darrell L. Bock, *A Theology of Luke and Acts: Biblical Theology of the New Testament*, ed. Andreas J. Köstenberger (Grand Rapids, MI: Zondervan, 2012), 28.

This admission serves to inform the reader of Luke's declared intent to provide an orderly account by which the Gospel narratives may be corroborated. Luke's Gospel therefore serves as a fitting witness for this reason. Darrell Bock explains: "An examination of Luke's use of his sources shows his general trustworthiness. Investigations into his descriptions of settings, customs, and locales reveal the same sensitivity. Luke is a first-class ancient historian, and most good ancient historians understood their task well."[61]

Luke was an historian of the highest order. Unlike the other apostles, Luke could not be rightly perceived as "uneducated and untrained" (Acts 4:13). Moreover, Luke's testimony uniquely offers the outside perspective of a Gentile, rather than the Jewish orientation that is common to the rest of the New Testament.

Despite these differences, Luke's witness does not contrast Matthew's, but rather serves to confirm it in nearly every regard. This parallel witness is found not only in content but even in structure, for only Luke's and Matthew's testimonies provide Jesus' genealogy—albeit, each traces a different lineage. Moreover, in similar fashion to Matthew, Luke's Gospel also closes with the commissioning of the eleven:

> Then He said to them, "Thus it is written, and thus it was necessary for the Christ to suffer and to rise from the dead the third day, and that repentance and remission of sins should be preached in His name to all nations, beginning at Jerusalem. And you are witnesses of these things. Behold, I send the Promise of My Father upon you; but tarry in the city of Jerusalem until you are endued with power from on high." (Luke 24:46-49)

---

[61] Bock, 43.

Following the pattern of Matthew's Gospel, observed in previous chapters, Luke's account of this commission emphasizes the following three elements: 1) the message—Christ's suffering and resurrection on the third day for the remission of sins to those who repent; 2) the recipients— all the nations to whom the message should be preached; and 3) the consequent—the abiding presence of the Holy Spirit, Whom Christ will send from the Father (thereby emphasizing the congruent work of the three Persons of the Trinity).

Similarly, this scene serves as the conclusion for Luke's Gospel. Luke continues his testimony in a second treatise to Theophilus (Acts 1:1; cf. Luke 1:3) where he no longer refers to the Eleven as "disciples," but by the new term: "apostles" (lit. "sent ones" τοῖς ἀποστόλοις). This deliberate change of terminology is consistent with the Eleven's new identity as those whom Christ commissioned to carry this new Gospel into "all the world" and unto "all the nations."

What was this new Gospel? Simply stated, it was the testimony of Jesus' life, death, burial, and resurrection for the remission of sins unto people of all nations. This Gospel carried with it a consequent—that as many as received these words received the gift of the Holy Spirit, which Jesus had promised near the end of His life, but especially communicated after His resurrection. Therefore, for the sake of clarity, this may best be referred to as His post-ascension ministry, as distinguished from His prior earthly ministry.

Jesus' Earthly Ministry

The previous chapters demonstrated that Jesus carried out two distinctly discernible ministries, complete with different messages and different outcomes. The first of these ministries was the declaration of the kingdom's imminence which was pronounced to Israel with the intended result that those Jews who were worthy of repentance would be delivered through the coming wrath (Matt 3:7-12; 7:15-27; 10:11-15). This message was most succinctly summed up by Matthew in the expression: "Repent, the kingdom of heaven is at hand" (Matt 3:1; 4:17; 10:7).

Although this exact phrase is not repeated in the testimony of any of the other Synoptic Gospels, Luke offers readers the very same conclusion by Jesus' own admission: "I must preach the kingdom of God...because for this purpose I have been sent" (Luke 4:43). Luke's testimony immediately follows this declaration by remarking that Jesus went about "preaching in the synagogues of Galilee" (Luke 4:44).

Similarly, Luke's Gospel plainly details the Germinal Commission: "Then He called His twelve disciples together and gave them power and authority over all demons, and to cure diseases. He sent them to preach the kingdom of God and to heal the sick" (Luke 9:1-2). It is only sometime after this first missionary endeavor that Luke records Jesus' disclosure to the Twelve that He would be betrayed, crucified, and rise again three days later (Luke 9:22)—the message which serves as the content of the Great Commission.

Luke further reveals that even after years of following Him and listening to all of His teachings,[62] the Twelve were so befuddled by the prospect of Jesus' death and resurrection that they were literally unable to apprehend it, even after He had repeated it to them a second time (Luke 9:43-44). Luke records that "they did not understand this saying, and it was hidden from them so that they did not perceive it; and they were afraid to ask Him about the saying" (Luke 9:45).

---

[62] Thomas and Gundry, 117.

Luke records Christ's sending out of seventy others to accomplish the work of the preaching of the Gospel of the kingdom (Luke 10:1-20), an event not specifically detailed in either of the other Synoptic Gospels.[63] On this occasion, He imparted Kingdom authority to all seventy, and commanded them, saying:

> "Whatever city you enter, and they receive you, eat such things as are set before you. And heal the sick there, and say to them, 'The kingdom of God has come near to you.' But whatever city you enter, and they do not receive you, go out into its streets and say, 'The very dust of your city which clings to us we wipe off against you. Nevertheless know this, that the kingdom of God has come near you.' But I say to you that it will be more tolerable in that Day for Sodom than for that city." (Luke 10:8-12)

In these words we see the very same pattern outlined in the Germinal Commission: content—"the kingdom of God has come near to you" (Luke 10:9); audience—Jews dispersed throughout the cities (Luke 10:1, 10, 13, 15; cf. 4:15-16); compliment—authority over sickness and demons (Luke 10:9, 17); and consequent—escape from the coming judgment (Luke 10:12-15). These elements defined the preaching of Jesus as well as His disciples during the time of His ministry on earth. They do not, however, characterize the ministry of the apostles after He ascended to His Father in heaven.

Before proceeding to Luke's witness concerning Jesus' post-ascension ministry, it is important to observe a conversation between Jesus and His disciples, which bears great significance to the Germinal Commission. The conversation occurs on the night of Jesus' arrest, sometime after having preached His final message to a Jewish audience.

---

[63] Thomas and Gundry, 135.

Here, in the private context of speaking to His disciples, over the Passover meal, He looks back to the missionary mandate which He had previously commission them:

> And He said to them, "When I sent you without money bag, knapsack, and sandals, did you lack anything?"
>
> So they said, "Nothing."
>
> Then He said to them, "But now, he who has a money bag, let him take it, and likewise a knapsack; and he who has no sword, let him sell his garment and buy one. For I say to you that this which is written must still be accomplished in Me: 'And He was numbered with the transgressors.' For the things concerning Me have an end."
>
> So they said, "Lord, look, here are two swords."
>
> And He said to them, "It is enough." (Luke 22:35-38)

What is most significant about this dialogue between Jesus and His disciples is the strong contrast (ἀλλὰ) that is made between the disciples' previous mission "then" (ὅτε ἀπέστειλα) and "now" (νῦν). Speaking to this point, Greek expositor Alexander Bruce offers the following insight:

> ὅτε ἀπέστειλα: the reference is to ix. 3, or rather, so far as language is concerned, to x. 4, which relates to the mission of the *seventy*. –ἄτερ as in ver. 6.–ver. 36. ἀλλὰ νῦν, but *now*, suggesting an emphatic contrast between past and present, or near future.[64]

Whereas in Matthew's Gospel, the contrast in messages was represented by the phrase: "From that time Jesus began…" (Matt 4:17; 16:21), here the same contrast appears but in different words. Matthew's

---

[64] Bruce, 1:628-629.

contrast highlighted the starting point of Jesus' preaching concerning the coming of the kingdom of heaven (Matt 4:17) and the message of His death and resurrection (Matt 16:21). Luke, on the other hand, contrasts the Germinal Commission with the particular events that will lead to His death and subsequent resurrection: "For I say to you that this which is written must still be accomplished in Me: 'And He was numbered with the transgressors.' For the things concerning Me have an end" (Luke 22:37). The principle difference between these two accounts is that Luke does not, at this point, make specific reference to the message, but only to the fulfillment of prophecy concerning His death, which must precede it.

This connection is not altogether missed by Luke. Before the close of his Gospel, Luke is careful to point to this fulfillment of prophecy as requisite for the commission that would necessarily follow:

> Then He said to them, "These are the words which I spoke to you while I was still with you, that all things must be fulfilled which were written in the Law of Moses and the Prophets and the Psalms concerning Me." And He opened their understanding, that they might comprehend the Scriptures.
>
> Then He said to them, "Thus it is written, and thus it was necessary for the Christ to suffer and to rise from the dead the third day, and that repentance and remission of sins should be preached in His name to all nations, beginning at Jerusalem. And you are witnesses of these things. Behold, I send the Promise of My Father upon you; but tarry in the city of Jerusalem until you are endued with power from on high." (Luke 24:44-48)

Jesus' Post-Ascension Ministry

The first example of the apostles carrying out the commission of the risen Lord, is given in the second chapter of Acts, where it is written: "Then Peter said to them, 'Repent, and let every one of you be baptized in the name of Jesus Christ for the remission of sins; and you shall receive the gift of the Holy Spirit. For the promise is to you and to your children, and to all who are afar off, as many as the Lord our God will call'" (Acts 2:38-39).

In remarking on the discontinuity of this evangelistic effort from that of John the Baptist, R. J. Knowling notes:

> John's baptism had been a baptism of repentance for the remission of sins, but the work of St. Peter and of his fellow-Apostles was no mere continuation of that of the Baptist, *cf.* xix 4, 5. Their baptism was to be ἐπὶ τῷ ὀνόματι Ἰ.Χ. St. Peter's address had been directed to the proof that Jesus was the Christ, and it was only natural that the acknowledgement of the cogency of that proof should form the ground of the admission to the Christian Church: the ground of admission to baptism was the recognition of Jesus as the Christ.[65]

This unique message—along with the unprecedented ministry of the Holy Spirit which accompanied it—characterized the preaching of Peter and the apostles on the Day of Pentecost and thereafter (Acts 3:13-16; 4:2, 10-12; 5:30-32; etc.). Conspicuously absent from the preaching of the apostles throughout the Book of Acts is the phrase "the kingdom of heaven is at hand." In all the sermons which Peter preached after Christ's ascension, the phrase is never spoken.

The predominant theme beginning on the Day of Pentecost and continuing throughout the preaching ministry of the apostles is the message of salvation in the name of Jesus, "for there is no other name under heaven given among men by which we must be saved" (Acts 4:12).

---

[65] R. J. Knowling, "The Acts of the Apostles" in *The Expositor's Greek Testament*, ed. by W. Robertson Nicoll, (repr. Grand Rapids, MI: Wm. B. Eerdmans, 1976), 2:91.

Moreover, where this name was preached, the message was signified by the presence of the Holy Spirit: "And when they had prayed, the place where they were assembled together was shaken; and they were all filled with the Holy Spirit, and they spoke the word of God with boldness" (Acts 4:31).

In addition to the conspicuous absence of the phrase "the kingdom of heaven is at hand," throughout the preaching of the apostles, is that there is no reference to Jesus Christ as "King." Instead, another title is repeated: "Savior" (Acts 5:31, 13:23). Though, in one instance Peter and the apostles declared: "The God of our fathers raised up Jesus whom you murdered by hanging on a tree. Him God has exalted to His right hand to be Prince and Savior, to give repentance to Israel and forgiveness of sins. And we are His witnesses to these things, and so also is the Holy Spirit whom God has given those who obey Him" (Acts 5:30-31).

Peter points to the crucifixion, the resurrection, and the exaltation of Christ, as well as to the corresponding witness of the Holy Spirit. These are distinguishing features of the Great Commission, and yet none of them are present in the Germinal Commission.

While some may object that Christ is referred to by the term "Prince" in this passage, it should be noted that the Greek word used here is ἀρχηγός, which is typically translated "leader," and is altogether different and unrelated to βασιλεύς, which is the word for "king." The latter term is the same root for kingdom, and is used throughout the New Testament to designate both "king" and "kingdom," whether earthly or heavenly.

To further clarify that Peter did not have kingdom authority in mind, but rather salvific authority, one need only look at how Peter used this same title for the Christ in a similar context. Previously, in preaching at Solomon's Porch, Peter declared: "But you denied the Holy One and the Just, and asked for a murderer to be granted to you, and killed the Prince of life, whom God raised from the dead, of which we are witnesses" (Acts 3:15).

It can be seen from this context that Peter referred to Jesus as τὸν ἀρχηγὸν τῆς ζωῆς or "the Author of Life." This title is comparable to that which the Apostle Paul would later use to refer to Christ as "the head of the body, the church, who is the beginning, the firstborn from the dead" (Col 1:18), wherein the same Greek word (ἀρχή) is used of Jesus "ὅς ἐστιν ἀρχή πρωτότοκος ἐκ τῶν νεκρῶν."

Concerning Peter's use of this term, expositor Eckhard Schnabel explains:

> Peter connects the title "Author of Life" with Jesus' resurrection. As in his Pentecost speech (2:24, 29-32), Peter affirms that God "raised" Jesus from the dead. His earlier affirmation that God "glorified" Jesus (v. 13) amounts to the same point, as Jesus' resurrection signified that he was "exalted" at the right hand of God (2:33). In 5:31 Peter and the apostles tell the Jewish leaders that God "exalted" Jesus at his right hand "as Leader and Savior" (ἀρχηγὸν καὶ σωτῆρα).[66]

This same presentation of the Christ, which Peter and the apostles delivered to the Jewish population at Pentecost, and thereafter, was afterward offered to the first Gentile converts at the house of Cornelius. On that occasion, Peter specified which commission he had been given, stating: "And He commanded us to preach to the people, and to testify that it is He who was ordained by God to be Judge of the living and the dead. To Him all the prophets witness that, through His name, whoever believes in Him will receive remission of sins" (Acts 10:42-43). However,

---

[66] Schnabel, *Acts*, 210-211.

Peter's declaration is not the only witness that is provided to the reader to reveal which commission he was fulfilling. Here the text reveals not only the commission, but the message: "through His name, whoever believes in Him will receive remission of sins," to the Gentile audience, and the consequent all confirm that Peter was fulfilling the Great Commission:

> While Peter was still speaking these words, the Holy Spirit fell upon all those who heard the word. And those of the circumcision who believed were astonished, as many as came with Peter, because the gift of the Holy Spirit had been poured out on the Gentiles also. For they heard them speak with tongues and magnify God.
>
> Then Peter answered, "Can anyone forbid water, that these should not be baptized who have received the Holy Spirit just as we *have?*" And he commanded them to be baptized in the name of the Lord. (Acts 10:44-48)

After Peter's preaching to the household of Cornelius, this same message would later be delivered to the Gentiles by the Apostle Paul. In fact, the same Gospel which God had appointed Peter to deliver to the Jews, He would afterward entrust to Paul for dissemination to the Gentiles (Gal 2:7-9).

The Witness of Paul

Although any consideration of the Apostle Paul's ministry and message has been almost entirely neglected in this study of the two commissions of Mathew's Gospel, its significance cannot be overstated. Paul's testimony most vividly declares the gospel which the apostles preached in the following words:

> I declare to you the gospel which I preached to you, which also you received and in which you stand, by which also you are

saved...that Christ died for our sins according to the Scripture, and that He was buried, and that He rose again the third day according to the Scriptures, and the He was seen by Cephas, then by the twelve. (1 Cor 15:1-5)

Paul's gospel is herein succinctly summed up to include the following points: the death of Christ and burial of Christ as prophesied in the Old Testament and His subsequent resurrection and appearance to the many eye-witnesses. This gospel message forms the foundation for Paul's preaching.

As previously demonstrated, this message was not only conspicuously absent from the public ministry of Jesus to the Jewish people, it was an altogether foreign concept to the disciples who had spent years under His teaching. Thus, it could not have been included in their message at the time they were sent out to preach to the lost sheep of the House of Israel in accordance with the Germinal Commission (Matt 10:5-8). Neither was it contained in the gospel which John the Baptist preached, for theirs was the same message: "the kingdom of heaven is at hand!"

Although Paul had no exclusive claim to this gospel, he nevertheless repeatedly used language to distinguish it from other gospels that were preached in his day, by use of the phrase: "my gospel" (Rom 2:16; 16:25; 2 Tim 2:8). This gospel, which Paul characterized as "his own" is declared in Scripture to be the one by which "God will judge the secrets of men by Jesus Christ" (Rom 2:16). Some readers may be agitated by the notion that God would judge men on the basis Paul's gospel; however, this should not be regarded so much as a statement of exclusion, than one of definition. Paul's gospel was also shared by the other apostles. The primary difference being the intended audience. The Apostle expresses this idea in his letter to the Galatians:

> When they saw that the gospel for the uncircumcised had been committed to me, as *the gospel* for the circumcised was to Peter (for He who worked effectively in Peter for the apostleship to the circumcised also worked effectively in me toward the Gentiles), and when James, Cephas, and John, who seemed to be pillars, perceived the grace that had been given to me, they gave me and Barnabas the right hand of fellowship, that we should go to the Gentiles and they to the circumcised. (Gal 2:7-9)

By Paul's own admission, he denies any distinction of gospel message. Rather, God had determined a distinction of the scope of the two apostles' respective ministries—Peter, a minister to the Jews, and Paul, a minister to the Gentiles. The end result of both ministries would be the same: "to create in Himself one new man from the two, thus making peace, and that He might reconcile them both to God in one body through the cross, thereby putting to death the enmity" (Eph 2:15-16).

In his letter to the Ephesians, Paul emphasizes this theme of reconciliation between Jew and Gentile and the breaking down of "the middle wall of separation" (Eph 2:14) between the two peoples, "for through Him we both have access by one Spirit to the Father" (Eph 2:18). Paul refers to this theme of reconciliation as a mystery, which had previously been unknown to both Jew and Gentile but now, at last, has been made plain.

> For this reason I, Paul, the prisoner of Christ Jesus for you Gentiles—if indeed you have heard of the dispensation of the grace of God which was given to me for you, how that by revelation He made known to me the mystery... which from the beginning of the ages has been hidden in God who created all things through Jesus Christ; to the intent that now the manifold wisdom of God might be made known by the church to the principalities and powers in the heavenly *places,* according to the eternal purpose which He accomplished in Christ Jesus our Lord. (Eph 3:1-3, 9-11)

The Apostle reveals that this is not to be understood as a new plan in God's unfolding work as much as it is a new phase in what God had purposed from the beginning. Therefore, this reconciliation of Jew and Gentile is "according to the eternal purpose" of God. Exegetical commentator Harold Hoehner is careful to make the following distinction:

> Care must be taken not to make Gentile believers a part of Israel...this is contrary to the whole point of Eph 2:11-22 where the "new person" is distinct from the nation Israel. Gentiles do not become Jews but rather Jews and Gentiles become "one new person." The church is not the new Israel but a distinct body of believers made up of believing Jews and Gentiles.[67]

Paul, a learned Hebrew scholar and self-described "Pharisee, the son of a Pharisee" (Acts 23:6, cf. Phil 3:5), had no prior knowledge of this eternal plan of God until it was revealed to Him by revelation from God. He elsewhere declared: "But I make known to you, brethren, that the gospel which was preached by me is not according to man. For I neither received it from man, nor was I taught *it*, but *it came* through revelation of Jesus Christ" (Gal 1:11-12).

What's even more remarkable is that this gospel which Paul had received by the Spirit of God was not one with which Peter appeared to have any great familiarity. In fact, it threatened to become a source of contention between the ministries of Peter and Paul, until at last, the Holy Spirit confirmed for Peter, James, and John, that the stewardship of the message of God's grace extended to the Gentiles had been uniquely conferred to Paul by the Holy Spirit (cf. Gal 2:9; Eph 3:1-3, 7-12).

---

[67] Harold W. Hoehner, *Ephesians: An Exegetical Commentary* (Grand Rapids, MI: Baker Academic, 2002), 447.

One must conclude that there would have been no occasion for contention between the preaching ministry of those who had walked with Jesus for over three years and that of the Apostle Paul if their message was the same. Moreover, if either party was in need of correction, one must surmise that those who had walked with Jesus and listened to His every message would be the ones doing the correction. Nevertheless, Scripture declares that Paul "did not yield submission even for an hour" to the other apostles for the sake of preserving "the truth of the gospel" (Gal 2:5) which God had entrusted to him.

Again, it must be stated that Paul's gospel was not exclusive to him, for it was the same gospel which God had entrusted to Peter and the other apostles to announce to the Jews. The fact remains, the message of the gospel which all of the apostles were given to preach was measured against the standard which was maintained by Paul as the steward of the mystery. Thus, Paul was operating within his capacity as steward of this mystery when he declared: "Now when Peter had come to Antioch, I withstood him to his face, because he was to be blamed...when I saw that they were not straightforward about the truth of the gospel" (Gal 2:11, 14).

On account of this, it may be seen that Paul rightly asserted: "God will judge the secrets of men by Jesus Christ, according to my gospel" (Rom 2:16). Moreover, he confirmed this in the following words:

> Now to Him who is able to establish you according to my gospel and the preaching of Jesus Christ, according to the revelation of the mystery kept secret since the world began but now made manifest, and by the prophetic Scriptures made known to all nations, according to the commandment of the everlasting God. (Rom. 16:25-26)

Finally, this "commandment of the everlasting God" to which the Apostle Paul refers at the close of his Epistle to the Romans is most reasonably understood to be that commission Christ gave to His disciples, directing them to carry the message of the efficacy of His life, death, and resurrection to all the nations. This is the message on which all of the Synoptic Gospels close (Matt 28:19-20; Mk 16:15-16; Luke 23:46-49). The response invoked by this Great Commission is what Luke chronicled in the Acts of the Apostles.

Conclusion

Although the term "Great Commission" refers to that specific directive of Jesus recorded at the end of Matthew's Gospel, it is quite certain that the missionary mandate was repeated multiple times and in a variety of ways over the course of the forty days in which He appeared to His disciples (Acts 1:3). McClain offers the following compilation, in his comparison of these complimentary narratives:

> [The disciples] witness would include the facts of His death and resurrection—that "it behooved Christ to suffer, and to rise from the dead" (Luke 24:46).
>
> In His name they were commissioned to preach "repentance and remission of sins...among all nations" (Luke 24:47); to "preach the gospel to every creature" (Mark 16:15); to "disciple all nations" (Matt. 28:19, lit.).
>
> In accomplishing this work the disciples were to follow a definite order of procedure: to Jerusalem first, then to all Judea, then to Samaria, and then to the uttermost part of the earth (Acts 1:8).
>
> Believers were to be fed (John 21:15-17), baptized, and taught to observe all that Christ had commended the first disciples (Matt. 28:19-20).

Unbelievers were to be warned of divine judgment: "he that believeth not shall be damned" (Mark 16:16).

In the accomplishment of this work, they would be empowered by the Holy Spirit (Acts 1:8), and the spiritual presence of Christ would be with them to the end of the age (Matt. 28:20).[68]

What is affirmed by this composite list is that the post-ascension message and ministry of Jesus were of a character entirely distinguishable from that which He conducted throughout His life. That earthly message of Jesus, which was also shared by His disciples during the period of His ministry, was one of declaring to the Jews the arrival of the Messianic King and the implications that would follow from His presence—namely, the arrival of the heavenly kingdom.

After Christ's ascension, He appeared to His disciples on multiple occasions to evidence His victory over the grave and to broadcast the enduring implications of that victory—namely, that all who would believe in Him would become recipients of the promise of the Holy Spirit, regardless of their national or religious heritage. It was not enough that the disciples retained this information for posterity, they were expressly commanded to share it with all the peoples of the earth, both near and far, and to signify that preaching with the act of baptizing believers into "the name of the Father and of the Son and of the Holy Spirit" (Matt 28:20).

---

[68] McClain, 392.

Ministry	Message	Audience	Intent	Outcome
Earthly (Matt 4:17-27:50; Luke 4:14-23:46)	The King is here, the Kingdom is near (Matt 4:17; Luke 4:43)	Jews (Matt 3:1, 5-8)	Israel's National Repentance (Matt 4:17; cf. 23:37-39)	Receive the Kingdom (Matt 5:1-12; 15:1-52; 20:1-16; cf. 20:20-23; 22:1-13)
Post-ascension (Matt 28; Luke 24; Acts 1ff)	Believe in the Lord and you will be saved (Acts 2:38-39; 16:31; Rom. 10:9; 1 Cor. 15:1-5)	All Nations (Matt 28:19; Acts 1:8)	Eternally Securing Believers (Rom 3:22-26; Heb 2:10; 5:9)	Receive the Holy Spirit (Acts 2:38; 10:42-48; 19:1-7; Rom 8:9-17)

Two Ministries – Table 4.1

CHAPTER 5
THEOLOGICAL IMPLICATIONS

God, who at various times and in various ways spoke in time past to the fathers by the prophets, has in these last days spoken to us by His Son. (Heb 1:1-2)

Common Views

A survey of Matthew's Gospel has provided sufficient background to understand two discernible missionary mandates where Christ sent His disciples to two different people groups with two evidently distinct messages. A closer look at these two commissions has revealed that each served a specific purpose for a distinct people at a particular time. A consideration of the analogous witness of both Luke and Paul has demonstrated that this perspective was not exclusive to Matthew's portrayal, but was also understood and corroborated by the apostles and prophets throughout the New Testament. The question that remains has to do with the theological implications of these two commissions for today's reader.

As stated in the introductory chapter of this book, there have historically been two distinct perspectives offered by covenantalists and dispensationalists regarding the Great Commission. The covenantalist view suggests that the Great Commission is a seamless extension of the missionary heart of God, expressed continuously throughout the entirety of the Old and New Testaments. While there has not been unanimous agreement among dispensationalists on a single view, the traditional dispensationalist position perceives of a commission of Christ that was more-or-less restricted to the apostles that were present in Galilee at the time of the utterance of those words, with no immediate bearing on the Christian church today. To what extent are either of these views confirmed or refuted by the exegetical analysis of the Gospel of Matthew provided in the previous chapters?

Continuous – Covenantal

The continuous view is one that is consistent with the covenantal understanding of Scripture, such as is common to the Reformed tradition. A leading proponent of this view, Michael Horton, summarizes it this way: "Covenant theology begins with continuity rather than discontinuity, not because of any a priori bias, but because Scripture itself moves from promise to fulfillment, not from one distinct program to another and then back again."[69] This concept is attractive because of its simplicity as well as its apparent consistency with the immutable character of God (Heb 13:8; Jas 1:17).

However, it may be too hasty a generalization to presume that because God's nature never changes neither does His message to man. To the contrary, Scripture is rife with seemingly discordant messages from God. For instance, beginning as early as the first chapter of Genesis, God

---

[69] Michael Horton, *God of Promise: Introducing Covenant Theology* (Grand Rapids, MI: Baker Books, 2006), 20.

created man and woman and prescribed them a diet that was to consist exclusively of the produce from the earth: "See I have given you every herb *that* yields seed which *is* on the face of all the earth, and every tree whose fruit yields seed; to you it shall be for food" (Gen 1:29). Sometime afterward, in the days of Noah, God prescribed a new diet for all the inhabitants of the earth: "Every living thing that lives shall be food for you. I have given you all things, even as the green herbs" (Gen 9:3). Later in history, during the days of Moses, God gave a restricted diet to the nation of Israel, while leaving the former diet in place for the remainder of earth's inhabitants. This diet included detailed regulations on which foods were clean and which were not (Lev 11).

While God never rescinded this diet for national Israel, He afterward made a startling declaration to Peter, once he became no longer distinguished as either Jew or Gentile but rather as a member of the New Creation in Christ: "Rise, Peter; kill and eat" (Acts 10:13). Peter's struggle with responding to this change in God's operation was made quite evident in his denial of the Lord's command. Peter appealed to the fact that he was faithfully keeping the Lord's prior instruction: "Not so, Lord! For I have never eaten anything common or unclean" (Acts 10:14). To which the Lord responded, "What God has cleansed you must not call common" (Acts 10:15). The Apostle's reluctance to thoroughly comprehend this change in God's operation is likely to have contributed to the challenges he would experience later in settings where he would share meals with Gentile believers, provoking Paul's rebuke (Gal 2:11-21).

This was not the first time the Apostle Peter was challenged by such changes in God's operation. As noted in chapter three, toward the end of Jesus' earthly ministry He "began to show His disciples that He must go to Jerusalem, and suffer many things from the elders and chief

priests and scribes, and be killed, and be raised the third day" (Matt
16:21). Peter's initial response was one of outright rejection (Matt 16:22).
On that occasion he provoked a chastening from Christ that makes Paul's
look mild by comparison: "Get behind Me, Satan! You are an offense to
Me, for you are not mindful of the things of God, but the things of men"
(Matt 16:23).

Elsewhere in Scripture, God can be clearly seen making changes in
His operation: "God, who at various times and in various ways spoke in
time past to the fathers by the prophets, has in these last days spoken to us
by His Son" (Heb 1:1-2). The implication of this passage is clear. God at
one time dealt with His people in one way but now He deals with them in
an altogether different manner. God does not change, but His operations
indeed do.

In acknowledgement of such changes, the prominent covenant
theologian, Louis Berkhof comments: "the New Testament dispensation
differs from that of the Old in that it is universal, that is, extends to all
nations."[70] Nowhere is this universal thrust of God to all nations more
evident than in the words of the Great Commission. Speaking specifically
to this end, Berkhof elaborates:

> Several important changes resulted from the accomplished work
> of Jesus Christ. The Church was divorced from the national life of
> Israel and obtained an independent organization. In connection
> with this the national boundaries of the Church were swept away.
> What had up to this time been a national Church now assumed a
> universal character. And in order to realize the ideal of world-wide

---

[70] Louis Berkhof, *Systematic Theology* (1939; repr. Grand Rapids, MI: Wm B.
Eerdmans Publishing Co., 1974), 300.

extension, it had become a missionary Church, carrying the gospel of salvation to all the nations of the world.[71]

It is demonstrated in this passage that Berkhof uses the term "church" far more broadly than some may find acceptable. Nevertheless, his message is made clear. The Church of the New Testament is a thing "divorced from the national life of Israel." It is an independent organization. Whereas the people of God previously had their identity wrapped up with a single earthly nation (Israel), God was now concerned with carrying out a new mission ("the gospel of salvation") to a new people ("all the nations of the world").

It should be noted that this is not the conclusion that is most typical of continuationists. Instead, covenantalists would generally favor a less divided structure to the Gospels. Dutch-Reformed theologian Herman Ridderbos offers the following commentary on the two commissions of Matthew:

> The first passage in this connection is about an incident during Jesus' stay in Galilee. It is the sending of the disciples mentioned in Matthew 10, Mark 6, and Luke 9, together with the sending of the seventy (-two) mentioned in Luke 10...already in this first mission the principal characteristic becomes visible of that which Jesus later entrusted to the disciples as a permanent and continuous charge, viz., preaching the gospel in word and deed. It is true that there is here no explicit question of the initial stage of the formation of a church. But Jesus does say that the disciples must go to the lost sheep of the house of Israel (Matt 10:6).[72]

---

[71] Berkhof, 571.

[72] Herman Ridderbos, *The Coming of the Kingdom*, ed. Raymond O. Zorn, trans. H. de Jongste (Philadelphia, PA: The Presbyterian and Reformed Publishing Company, 1975), 369-371.

It can be seen here that Ridderbos takes great effort to blur the lines of distinction between the two commissions. This type of approach is much more normative in the covenantal perspective. As he goes on, Ridderbos can even be seen taking the misstep of reading into the first preaching of the coming kingdom that which is nowhere to be found in the text:

> All this reveals the character of the first mission of the disciples as a sifting and a gathering together of the true people of God. Their coming brings peace (*eirēnē*), i.e. salvation in the most comprehensive sense of the word. For their having been "sent" by Jesus stamps their blessing, not simply as a wish, but characterizes it as a gift which is either accepted or rejected. Their mission makes manifest those who shall go free on the judgment day; it gathers together the true sheep of the house of Israel.[73]

Ridderbos concludes that the disciples' declaration "Peace be to this house" (Luke 10:5) is somehow compatible with the salvation that comes when one receives forgiveness of sins through the shed blood of Christ upon the cross. However, any such comparison cannot be said to emerge from an exegetical study of the biblical text. Moreover, to speculate that the pronouncement of Christ's coming kingdom was to "manifest those who shall go free on judgment day"[74] could result only from a reading of the latter commission into the former. Despite the protest of covenantalists, the continuity view may actually be rooted in more of an "a priori bias"[75] than some might be comfortable to admit.

---

[73] Ridderbos, 371.

[74] Ibid.

[75] Horton, 20.

The tension that exists between these two commissions is not one which emerges from a theological construct. It does not require a dispensational or discontinuous bias in order to make more of these commissions than is plainly evident in the text. To the contrary, it takes tremendous effort to minimize the distinctions. Such effort must inevitably move away from the plain language of the text and toward an abstract-conceptual, and more ethereal view.

The great lengths to which some Bible expositors have gone in an attempt to create a more harmonious transition from the ministry of John the Baptist, which Jesus and His disciples carried-on, and that message which was preached by them thereafter is quite remarkable. Whether deliberately, or as a subconscious result of an a priori bias, this dissonance—so stark and undeniable from the text—has, nevertheless gone overlooked by many exegetes and expositors. One such example from *The Expositor's Greek Commentary* appears as follows:

> μετανοεῖτε, Repent. That was John's great word. Jesus used it also when He began to preach, but His distinctive watchword was *Believe*. The two watchwords point to different conceptions of the kingdom. John's kingdom was an object of awful dread, Jesus' of glad welcome. The message of the one was legal, of the other evangelistic.[76]

Later, when this same expositor is confronted with the precise verbiage concerning Jesus (Matt 4:17), he gives the following admission:

> κηρύσσειν, the same word as in describing the ministry of the Baptist (iii, I). And the message is the same—μετανοεῖτε, etc. "Repent, for the kingdom of heaven is at hand." The same in *word* but not in *thought*, as will appear soon. It may seem as if the

---

[76] Bruce, "The Synoptic Gospels," 79.

evangelist meant to represent Jesus as simply taking up and continuing the arrested ministry of the Baptist. So He was in form and to outward appearance, but not in spirit.[77]

To parse out the "thought" of Jesus from His plainly declared "word" is a precarious thing, to be sure. This is likely what drove the expositor to italicize the very words. After all, a spoken (or written) word is nothing more than a mere expression of one's unspoken thought. To ascribe meaning to the thought beyond that which is expressed through the word is to move beyond exegesis. Even to those who would like for it to be otherwise, the conclusion is unavoidable: John the Baptist's message and Jesus' message were "the same in *word*." If "it may seem as if the evangelist meant to represent Jesus as simply taking up and continuing the arrested ministry of John the Baptist" it is because the biblical text presents it so.

Discontinuous – Dispensational

If the traditional covenantal perspective concerning the two commissions is fraught with challenges, it should be noted that the traditional dispensational perspective is even more egregious. While no singular consensus exists among dispensationalists concerning the discontinuity among the commissions of Christ, the view which served to distinguish the classical dispensational perspective was one which asserted that Matthew's Great Commission was not a directive to be carried-out by the Christian church today. This position was popularized by men such as John Nelson Darby, James M. Gray, William L. Pettington, Arno C. Gaebelin, and E. W. Bullinger. In his book entitled *Things That Differ: The*

---

[77] Bruce, "The Synoptic Gospels," 92.

Fundamentals of Dispensationalism, Cornelius R. Stam included the illustration below as part of an introduction to his chapter entitled, "The So-Called Great Commission":

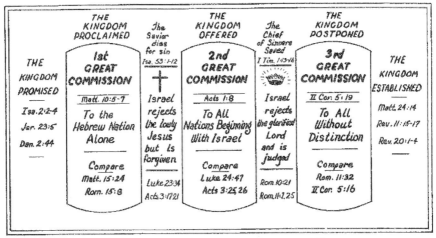

Illustration 5.1 – "The So-Called Great Commission"[78]

Stam's illustration identifies three separate commissions, all of which are referred to by the term "Great Commission," and yet none of which include the Matthew 28:19-20 directive. Although Luke 24:47 is referenced in this illustration, the particular view depicted here would not regard this as compatible with the commission of Matthew 28:19-20. This view is elsewhere expressed in an admission of Darby: "Luke's Commission is evidently different [from Matthew's]...The Matthew

---

[78] Cornelius R. Stam, *Things That Differ: The Fundamentals of Dispensationalism* (Chicago: IL: Berean Bible Society, 1985), 168.

commission was never carried into execution in Scripture, but merely dropped. The Acts are entirely the Luke commission."[79]

As previously mentioned, there has not been a singularly accepted view among dispensationalists. Nevertheless, there has been general agreement that discontinuity existed not merely amidst the two commissions of Matthew's Gospel, but also across a multitude of evangelistic assertions expressed throughout the life of Christ and in His post-ascension ministry. So many conflicting ideas have been promoted by dispensationalists concerning which "commissions" are for which purpose, and to whom, that dispensational expositors have not only contradicted one another, but at times even themselves. In one place, Darby speaks repeatedly of "Luke's commission," differing from Matthew's[80] while in another place he refutes himself, stating that: "Luke is different. There is not properly a commission."[81]

This disagreement amongst dispensationalists over which of the multitude of commissions expressed in the Gospels and Acts differ from which is acknowledged in the following admission of Stam: "Comparatively few Christian people are aware of the fact that our spiritual leaders have never agreed as to which of the five passages referred to above embodies *our* commission for today, but the disagreement has been sharp."[82] It is worth noting that the five passages which Stam refers

---

[79] John Nelson Darby, *Notes and Comments on Scripture* (repr. Germany: Blijhamsterstraat, 1971), 4:303.

[80] Darby, 4:303.

[81] John Nelson Darby, *Notes and Comments on Scripture* (repr. Germany: Blijhamsterstraat, 1971), 5:177.

[82] Stam, 170.

to include Matthew 28:20, Mark 16:16-18, Luke 24:47, Acts 1:8, and John 20:22,23, and yet it excludes what is depicted in illustration 5.1 under the heading "3rd Great Commission" (2 Cor 5:19). Therefore, according to Stam there are at least six different commissions.

Whereas dispensationalists have differed regarding the number of commissions and the specific parameters of each, a theme which characterized the majority view was that the Great Commission articulated at the close of Matthew's Gospel does not pertain to the Christian endeavor. Arno C. Gaeblin describes it in these words:

> He gives them the great commission to proclaim the kingdom world-wide...This is the *Kingdom* commission. In Luke xxiv we have the proper Christian mission. A time is coming when this [Matthew 28] great commission here will be carried out by a remnant of Jewish disciples, who are represented by the eleven.[83]

Later Gaebelein goes on to quote Darby:

> The accomplishment of the commission here in Matthew has been interrupted, but there is the promise to be with those who went forth in it to the end of the age. Nor do I doubt it will be so. This testimony will go forth to the nations before the Lord comes. 'The Brethren' will carry it to warn the nations. The commission was given, but we find no accomplishment of it. It connects the testimony with the Jewish remnant owned by a risen Lord of all, with the earth and His earthly directions, and for the present it has in fact given place to a heavenly commission, and the church of God.[84]

---

[83] Gaebelein, 622.

[84] Ibid., 623.

In response to this, Gaebelein concludes: "How wonderful and harmonious is the Word of God."[85] The "harmony" which he refers to has to do with the continuity of the Great Commission of chapter 28 with the rest of Matthew's Gospel. This in fact is the very place where readers should not seek to find continuity, but instead discontinuity.

In summary, the traditional dispensational understanding of Matthew 28 is one which sees Christ progressing along the very same lines as He did throughout His earthly ministry. Darby, *et al.* perceived Jesus' post-ascension directive to be one which was presented to the eleven for the purpose of continuing that same work which He had given them to carry out some three years prior, "The kingdom of heaven is at hand" (Matt 10:7). The only real difference they would see between the two commissions of Matthew is that previously He insisted "Do not go into the way of the Gentiles, and do not enter a city of the Samaritans. But go rather to the lost sheep of the house of Israel" (Matt 10:5, 6) whereas later He broadened the target audience to include "all the nations" (Matt 28:19). In this regard, though admittedly not in many others, one might see parallels to the continuous-covenantal view.

The discontinuity within this dispensational view is found between the pronouncement of Christ's words in Matthew's Great Commission and that which the apostles actually acted upon, as Darby notes: "The Matthew commission was never carried into execution in Scripture, but merely dropped."[86] One might wonder if this is what would bring Darby to drop the word "Great" in referring to Matthew's

---

[85] Gaebelein, 623.

[86] Darby, 4:303.

commission, as well as why Matthew 28 is omitted by Stam (in illustration 5.1), whereas three other passages are given the designation "1st," "2nd," and "3rd Great Commission."

While it is noteworthy that the dispensational view acknowledges certain discontinuities between the preaching of the kingdom, which was originally restricted to the Jewish people, and the preaching of the apostles, which began in Jerusalem at Pentecost and rapidly spread throughout the known world, there is little else commendable about this position. It is not hard to see from this interpretation how many have come to regard dispensationalism as a super-imposed theological construct that is guilty of unnaturally forcing upon Scripture a meaning that is not inherent to the text.

Conclusion

As it has been demonstrated in the previous chapters, Matthew has provided sufficient reason for the reader to conclude that there exists both continuity and discontinuity in his Gospel narrative, and that these two are not mutually exclusive. In an attempt to find harmony in the biblical narrative readers need not continue minimizing the tension that exists between the preaching of Christ's earthly ministry and that carried out by the apostles. The continuity is inherent in the text. Moreover, it should be regarded as no less egregious to read continuity into the text where it does not exist than it is to commit the dispensationalists' error of imposing discontinuity on the biblical text where it does not exist. The student of Scripture must always be a diligent exegete whose chief goal is to draw the meaning out from the text, as God has placed it there.

The covenantalist will find it arduous to demonstrate that the Great Commission at the close of Matthew's Gospel is a seamless

continuation of God's work committed to His people throughout the Old
Testament. Similarly, the dispensationalist is no less mistaken to
demonstrate from Scripture that making disciples and baptizing them into
the name of the Father and of the Son and of the Holy Spirit is not a work
which the early church was to carry out until the end of the age rather
than merely at the end of the age. Rather, it is a reasonable conclusion,
and one which emerges from the text, to see the post-resurrection
commissions as presented in each of the Synoptics as harmonious.
Differences that emerge from a comparison of these accounts should be
understood in light of the fact that Jesus made numerous appearances to
His disciples over the forty days subsequent to His resurrection during
which He gave them instruction.

View	Germinal	Great	Apostolic Ministry
Covenantal - Continuous	Continuous	Continuous	Continuous
Dispensational - Discontinuous	Continuous	Continuous	Discontinuous
Preferred - Discontinuous	Continuous	Discontinuous	Discontinuous

Commission Continuity – Table 5.1

CHAPTER 6
CONCLUSION

> Be diligent to present yourself approved to God, a worker who does not need to be ashamed, rightly dividing the word of truth. (2 Tim 2:15)

The Great Commission is among the most identifiable teachings of Jesus Christ. It is the only communication of the resurrected Lord conveyed by each of the four Gospel writers (Matt 28:18-20; Mark 16:15-16; Luke 24:46-49; John 20:21-22) and reiterated in the Acts of the Apostles (Acts 1:8; 26:13-18). Christ's command to His disciples to "Go into all the world and preach the gospel to every creature" (Mark 16:15), has come to be generally regarded as the evangelical mandate of the Christian church and serves to distinguish that branch of Christianity commonly referred to in the modern church by the term "Evangelical." In *A Biblical Theology of Missions*, George W. Peters asserts:

> The Great Commission...has far-reaching implications. It constitutes an identification of the believers with Christ in accomplishing the divine purpose as unfolded in the missionary thrust of the Old Testament and incarnated in the Lord. It is the command to preach the gospel to every creature, the marching orders to evangelize the world, the divine authorization to be ambassadors of Christ to every nation of the world. The

cumulative force of this reiterated command is evident, leaving no doubt in the mind of the believing and obeying disciple of Jesus Christ that the evangelization of the world is the unquestionable will and plan of the Lord. It is the divine imperative written in bold letters into the nature of Christianity and defined in a plain commandment by the Lord Himself.[87]

If the Great Commission is so central to the activities of the Christian church today, how is it that so many would misperceive it and even go so far as to say that it does not speak to the mission of the church, whatsoever? The answer to this question lies in the stark discontinuity that is so apparent in Matthew's Gospel. Any reader who objectively engages in an inductive reading of Matthew's Gospel and juxtaposes it against a reading of the Acts of the Apostles and the Epistles of Paul must reckon with the issue of continuity and discontinuity.

This point may be demonstrated in the following words of one of the most popular evangelical commentaries from a reformed perspective:

> When surrounded by multitudes of eager listeners, of every class and from all quarters, and solemnly seated on a mountain on purpose to teach them for the first time the great leading principles of His kingdom, why, it may be asked, did our Lord not discourse to them in such strains as these:—"God so loved the world, that He gave His only begotten Son, that whosoever believeth in Him should not perish, but have everlasting life;" "Come unto me, all ye that labour and are heavy laden, and I will give you rest," etc.? While the absence of such sayings from this His first great Discourse startles some to whom they are all-

---

[87] George W. Peters, *A Biblical Theology of Missions* (Chicago, IL: Moody Press, 1984), 178.

precious, it emboldens others to think that evangelical Christians make too much of them, if not entirely misconceive them.[88]

These remarks concerning the character of Jesus' earthly preaching speak volumes to this issue: Should Evangelicals be found guilty of making more out of John 3:16 than is rightly intended, since Jesus never once spoke it? Are Christians today taking the preaching of the Gospel unto salvation much further than Jesus ever did?

It is not necessary to suppress the tension that arises from such questions. The answer is simple. Christians *are* guilty of taking the evangelistic invitation much further than Jesus ever did. At the same time it is not wrong to say that they are taking it a further than He intended. The question may even be rightly asked whether it has yet been taken far enough.

A survey of Matthew's Gospel has provided sufficient background to understand two discernible missionary mandates where Christ sent His disciples to two different people groups with two evidently distinct messages. A closer look at these two commissions has revealed that each served a specific purpose for a distinct people at a particular time. A consideration of the analogous witness of Luke has demonstrated that this message was not exclusive to Matthew's Gospel—although undoubtedly, Matthew expressed it best. A survey of Matthew's Gospel has provided sufficient background for understanding the two discernible missionary mandates whereby Christ sent His disciples to two divergent people groups with two evidently distinct messages.

---

[88] Robert A. Jamieson, A. R. Fausset, and David Brown, *A Commentary on the Old and New Testaments* (1871; repr. Peabody, MA: Hendrickson Publishers, 2002), Vol. 3, 24.

Concerning these two commissions, the following can be concluded: the former was given during Jesus' life and mirrored His ministry which was directed at the House of Israel. The latter was given after Jesus had ascended from the tomb and attested to the efficacy of His death and resurrection, resulting in the abiding and yet unseen operation of the Holy Spirit among all nations. This former message characterized the long-awaited Messianic expectations of the nation of Israel. This latter message has characterized the Evangelical spirit of the Christian Church and has motivated the fervor that has driven missionary endeavors unto the ends of the earth.

Christians are entirely justified in seeking to carry-out the second of the two apostolic imperatives, known as the Great Commission. They are not in error in preaching that same message which the apostles preached concerning the life, death, resurrection of Jesus Christ. Neither are they wrong to carry the message of eternal life which issues from the abiding presence of the Holy Spirit unto everyone who places saving-faith in Jesus Christ. Moreover, water baptism serves as the signification of that unseen work of God whereby God baptizes the believer into Christ by means of the Spirit (1 Cor 12:13).

Whether Christians are remiss in not preaching that message concerning the coming Kingdom which Christ will bring with Him when He appears (Matt 24:30; Acts 1:11; 2 Thess 1:9-10; 2 Tim 4:1) is a matter not addressed in this brief study. Further work can be done in exploring this particular concern. Suffice it to say, in order for such a dialogue to occur, the nature of each distinct commission and its corresponding gospel message must first be rightly perceived, and this necessitates that the Scripture must first be rightly divided.

APPENDIX

A Conversation with Dr. Mark Strauss
Professor of New Testament, Bethel Seminary

The conversation below stemmed from a review of this work by Mark Strauss. It occurred to me that his reactions to this book are probably not atypical of the kind of responses many evangelical readers may have when presented with the contrasts contained here. With his gracious permission I have included both his questions and my responses to those questions to provide the reader with a more personal connection to the ideas behind the text.

Fazio: I want to thank you for your review of this book. I want you to know that the time you have taken to review and offer some initial reflections are immensely meaningful. In one instance, at least, you have spared me the embarrassment of sending to print an irresponsible and unqualified (moreover, an erroneous) statement. That, in itself, is invaluable to me. Furthermore, your comments have helped to provide me with the kind of reaction that many readers may have in response to the tension that I believe emerges from the text of Matthew's Gospel.

Please see my response to your specific questions below. To make a general statement in response to your claim:

> "Perhaps I'm misreading you, but the thesis seems to me akin to the Classical Dispensational perspective that the kingdom of God was offered to Israel, but was rejected and so postponed. So the message of the apostles and Paul's message is a different one, concerning the cross, but not the kingdom."

I would like to suggest that you are, perhaps reading more into the text than what I have placed there. I understand that the arguments may sound reminiscent of classical dispensational arguments, however, I have not drawn these conclusions in my text. Rather, I have merely observed that the message which Jesus presented to the Jews is explicitly framed in the biblical text using certain language that is conspicuously absent from the ministry of the disciples. I do not overstate this—though I acknowledge that classically this statement has been overstated by dispensationalists. At the same time, I do not shy away from these observations merely because others may have drawn certain conclusions from such overstatements.

Specific Questions:

"He sent His disciples to two different people groups with two very different messages." p. 2

"To be more precise, Jesus was in fact preaching the gospel, however that gospel differed in content from the one which Peter and the apostles preached at Pentecost and thereafter." p. 26

Strauss: Ironside's statement on this page that Jesus did not preach the gospel in the Sermon on the Mount seems to me blatantly wrong. The Gospel writers make it explicitly clear that Jesus' message is "the gospel" (Matt. 4:23; 9:35; 11:5, etc.).

Fazio: I would like to offer a statement that should help clarify my position: "Difference does not necessitate opposition any more than similarity necessitates identity." Admittedly, my focus in this section is on the distinction between gospels, rather than the similarity. I make it my aim to affirm that: "Jesus was in fact preaching the gospel" but that His "good news" differed in content to Peter's and Paul's "good news," which was preached only after Calvary, and is clearly discernable through the messages which are explicitly stated in the text. In this regard, I take exception with Ironside's remarks, stating that his conclusions are "perhaps too broad a statement" before concluding that "Jesus was in fact preaching the gospel."

> "However, the ideas expressed in these verses are undeniably different from those which Jesus preached throughout the course of His ministry." p. 44

Strauss: This context is about going to the Gentiles. But Jesus said things like "many will come from the east and the west, and will take their places at the feast with Abraham, Isaac and Jacob in the kingdom of heaven. But the subjects of the kingdom will be thrown outside" (Matt. 8:11-12). This is surely a reference to the Gentile mission.

Fazio: I agree that throughout even the Old Testament the Gentile inclusion in God's ultimate redemptive plan is in view, and this is similarly suggested by passages such as the one you've provided above. Nevertheless, I would contend that this fact does not make the statement which you referenced above any less true: The ideas expressed in these verses: "Do not go to the Gentiles" (10:5) and "I was sent only to the lost sheep of the House of Israel" (15:24) stand in stark contrast to those communicated at the close of Matthew's Gospel "Go into all the world...make disciples of all nations" (28:19-20).

"In contrast to the former message which Jesus and His disciples preached, this one carries every bit as much significance to the Gentile as it does to the Jew..." [emphasis added by Strauss] p. 47

Strauss: But doesn't Jesus' preaching of the kingdom also relate to Gentiles, as noted above?

Fazio: I do not believe that Jesus' cursory allusions to Gentiles in the kingdom—some of which occur in parabolic teachings (cf. Matt 13)—contradict the statement that His teaching message, which is defined by the phrase "Repent, for the Kingdom of heaven is at hand" and elaborated in the Sermon on the Mount, does not have the inclusion of the Gentiles in view. For instance, when I begin sharing the Gospel with someone, I may begin by asking some worldview questions. My end goal in view is to bring them to Christ, but it is entirely possible that throughout our entire conversation I do not even once reference the name of Christ. Jesus' ability to peer beyond the cross does not betray the expressed intent of His earthly ministry: "I have not come except for the lost sheep of the House of Israel" (15:24). At the risk of oversimplification, I would put it most succinctly: "Jesus' earthly ministry was for the Jews, but His death was for all men."

"That is to say, the message which Jesus, John the Baptist, and the Twelve had once preached, never found its way into the preaching of the early church..." p. 49

Strauss: Is this true? Paul refers to Jesus' teaching on divorce (1 Cor. 7), etc. and assumes it relates directly to the church.

Fazio: I intend throughout the book to clarify the content of "the message which Jesus, John the Baptist, and the Twelve preached" (see chart on pg. 41). The content of this message I have defined: "The Kingdom of heaven is at hand" (cf. 3:1; 4:17, 23; 10:7). I did not mean to suggest that nothing Jesus ever said in His earthly ministry was ever referenced by the apostles after His death (cf. 1 Cor 11:23-26 for the institution of the Lord's Supper). To do this would be utterly irresponsible. This was not my aim. I can see how a cursory perusal of the text may have revealed this to be the case, and I would genuinely hope that a more thorough reading would make this point clear, otherwise, I have failed in my chief aim.

> "The gospel had effectively shifted from: 'Go and tell the Jews that the kingdom is at hand' to 'Go and tell the world that I have been crucified and have risen again!'" p. 49

Strauss: But, as noted above, Paul speaks about the message of the cross as the message of the kingdom of God (both in Acts and in his epistles)

Fazio: Agreed. I have not made the claim in this work that the message of the cross is any way opposed to the message of the kingdom of God. Rather, I have suggested that the content of Jesus' preaching, which is also mirrored in the preaching of John the Baptist and of the commissioning of the twelve during Jesus' earthly ministry, was: "Repent, for the kingdom of heaven is at hand." Moreover, I emphasize that the message that Christians are given to preach today is best expressed in the crucifixion, burial, and resurrection of Jesus Christ (1 Cor 15:1-5). Once more, I nowhere imply that the message of Christ's crucifixion and resurrection stands in opposition or in contradiction to the message of the kingdom.

In fact, I would argue that it is integral (though I do not do so in this book).

> "The former was to be signified by the working of miracles, the latter was to be signified by the abiding presence of the Sending Agent." p. 61

Strauss: But the mission to the Gentile also involved miracles (throughout Acts and in Paul's letters).

Fazio: I need to take the opportunity to thank you for your critical review. I thoroughly appreciate each of these points you've raised...The mission to the Gentiles indeed did involve miracles. I do not mean to deny this. Once more, I believe I should remark that: "Difference does not necessitate opposition any more than similarity necessitates identity." Throughout this book I make mention of both the similarities and the distinctions. I believe that in recent centuries, covenantalists have erred on the side of over-emphasizing the similarities to the exclusion of the distinctions, and that on the other side, dispensationalists have erred by over-emphasizing the distinctions to the exclusion of the similarities. Both are necessary and should not be avoided. Admittedly, in the Christian church today, Christians tend to err on the side of an over-emphasis on the similarities, and there are very few voices seeking to draw any attention whatsoever to the distinctions. Therefore, it is my aim in this book to do so. However, I do not mean to do so at the expense of the similarities. Though it is also presented in that type of false-dilemma.

> "...Jesus carried out two distinctly discernible ministries, complete with different messages and different outcomes." p. 66

Strauss: This, as I've said before, seems to me fundamentally mistaken.

Fazio: This statement expresses the heart of this book. If you truly see no "distinctly discernable ministries" and no "different messages" with "different outcomes" then I would imagine you would see very little value in this book. It is my aim to suggest that the verses which I provided and the argument which I have offered in this book do reveal that Jesus' earthly ministry, which was admittedly directed toward a single people group had in view the national repentance of the Jewish people and their acceptance of the Jewish Messiah as King, along with His accompanying kingdom. The phrases which I believe demonstrate this best are the temporal markers which Matthew provides in His Gospel: "From that time Jesus began to preach and to say, 'Repent, for the kingdom of heaven is at hand'" (4:17), and "From that time Jesus began to show to His disciples that He must go to Jerusalem, and suffer many things from the elders and chief priests and scribes, and be killed, and be raised the third day" (16:21). To sum it up succinctly:

Two ministries: to the House of Israel / to all nations

Two messages: national repentance of Israel / belief in Christ

Two outcomes: acceptance of the Kingdom / identity in Christ

I don't offer these as competing ideas, but simply as different ideas. If you do not acknowledge that any such distinction exists then I understand your reluctance to offer an affirmation of this work. I believe it is common for Christians to pre-suppose certain conclusions from these distinctions, and therefore to suppress their acknowledgement of their existence. I aim in this work not to draw conclusions such as: these two ministries/messages/outcomes stand in opposition to one another. Rather, I simply aim to acknowledge that these tensions exist and must be confronted rather than shied away from.

Endorsement

In this volume James Fazio wrestles with the puzzling fact that Matthew's Jesus first tells his disciples *not* to take his message of the kingdom to the Gentiles (10:5) and tells the Canaanite woman that, "I was only sent to the lost sheep" (15:24). Only after his atoning work on the cross does he command the gospel to go to all nations (28:18-20). Did Jesus' plans change? Was the kingdom that was offered to Israel different from that proclaimed by Paul and the apostles in Acts and the Epistles? What *was* Jesus offering Israel when he announced the kingdom (if indeed he already had the cross in mind)? Without necessarily siding with classical dispensationalism (which claims the kingdom was postponed because of Israel's rejection), Fazio raises important questions that every responsible exegete of the Gospels must engage with. This volume challenged me again to think through these critical issues.

Mark Strauss

BIBLIOGRAPHY

Barbieri, Louis A. "Matthew." In *The Bible Knowledge Commentary of the New Testament*, edited by John F. Walvoord and Roy B. Zuck, 13-94. Colorado Springs, CO: Chariot Victor Publishing, 1999.

Barnes, Albert. *Barnes' Notes on the New Testament*. 1972. Reprint, Grand Rapids, MI: Kregel Publications 1962.

Berkhof, Louis. *Systematic Theology*. 1939. Reprint, Grand Rapids, MI: Wm B. Eerdmans Publishing Co., 1974.

Bock, Darrell L. *A Theology of Luke and Acts: Biblical Theology of the New Testament*. Edited Andreas J. Kostenberger. Grand Rapids, MI: Zondervan, 2012.

Bruce, Alexander Balmain. "The Synoptic Gospels." In *The Expositor's Greek Testament*, edited by W. Robertson Nicoll, 61-340. Vol 1. 1974. Reprint. Grand Rapids, MI: Wm. B. Eerdmans, 1976.

Carson, D. A. *Exegetical Fallacies*. 2nd ed. Grand Rapids, MI: Baker Academic, 1996.

———. "Matthew." In *Expositor's Bible Commentary: With the New International Version*, edited by Frank Gaebelein, 3-599. Vol 8. Grand Rapids, MI: Zondervan Publishing House, 1984.

Constable Thomas L. "Notes on Matthew." *Expository Notes*. 2013 Ed. Sonic Light. Accessed March 13, 2013. http://www.soniclight.com/constable/notes/pdf/matthew.pdf

Darby, John Nelson. *Notes and Comments on Scripture*. Vol. 4. Reprint, Germany: Blijhamsterstraat, 1971.

Darby, John Nelson. *Notes and Comments on Scripture*. Vol. 5. Reprint, Germany: Blijhamsterstraat, 1971.

Feinberg, John S. *Continuity and Discontinuity: Perspectives on the Relationship Between the Old and New Testaments*. Wheaton, IL: Crossway Books, 1988.

Gaebelein, Arno C. *The Gospel of Matthew: An Exposition*. 1910. Reprint, New York: Publication Office, Our Hope, 1961.

Hendriksen, William. *Exposition of the Gospel According to Matthew*. New Testament Commentary 1. Grand Rapids, MI: Baker Academic, 1981.

Hindson, Edward, and James Borland. *The Gospel of Matthew: The King is Coming*. Twenty-First Century Biblical Commentary. Edited by Mal Couch. Chattanooga, TN: AMG Publishers, 2006.

Hoehner, Harold W. *Ephesians: An Exegetical Commentary*. Grand Rapids, MI: Baker Academic, 2002.

Horton, Michael. *God of Promise: Introducing Covenant Theology*. Grand Rapids, MI: Baker Books, 2006.

Ironside, H. A. *Matthew*. An Ironside Expository Commentary. 1920. Reprint, Grand Rapids, MI: Kregel Publications, 2005.

Jamieson, Robert, A. R. Fausset, and David Brown. *A Commentary on the Old and New Testaments: Matthew-Revelation*. Vol. 3. 1871. Reprint, Peabody, MA: Hendrickson Publishers, 2002.

Kent Jr., Homer A. *Jerusalem to Rome: Studies in the Book of Acts*. 1972. Reprint, Grand Rapids, MI: Baker Book House, 2000.

Knowling, R. J. "The Acts of the Apostles." In *The Expositor's Greek Testament*, edited by W. Robertson Nicoll, 49-554. Vol 2. 1974.

Reprint, Grand Rapids, MI: Wm. B. Eerdmans Publishing Co., 1976.

Ladd, George Eldon. "Matthew." In *The Biblical Expositor*, edited by Carl F H. Henry, 23-72. Vol. 3. 1960. Reprint, Grand Rapids, MI: Baker Books, 1994.

MacArthur, John. *Matthew 24-28*. MacArthur New Testament Commentary. Chicago, IL: Moody Bible Institute, 1989.

McClain, Alva J. *The Greatness of the Kingdom: An Inductive Study of the Kingdom of God*. 1959. Reprint, Winona Lake, IN: BMH Books, 1992.

Moulton, James Hope. *Prolegomena*. Vol 1. *A Grammar of New Testament Greek*. Edinburgh: T. & T. Clark, 1908. Accessed February 16, 2013. http://faculty.gordon.edu/hu/bi/ted_hildebrandt /new_testament_greek/ text/moulton-grammarntgreek.pdf

Osborne, Grant R. *Matthew*. Exegetical Commentary on the New Testament 1. Edited by Clinton E. Arnold. Grand Rapids, MI: Zondervan, 2010.

Peters, George W. *A Biblical Theology of Missions*. Chicago, IL: Moody Press, 1984.

Ridderbos, Herman. *The Coming of the Kingdom*. Edited by Raymond O. Zorn. Translated by H. de Jongste. Philadelphia, PA: The Presbyterian and Reformed Publishing Company, 1975.

Schnabel, Eckhard J. *Acts*. Exegetical Commentary on the New Testament 5, edited Clinton E. Arnold. Grand Rapids, MI: Zondervan, 2012.

Stam, Cornelius R. *Things That Differ: The Fundamentals of Dispensationalism*. Chicago, IL: Berean Bible Society, 1985.

ph H. *Thayer's Greek-English Lexicon of the New Testament.* 1896. print, Peabody, MS: Hendrickson Publishers, 2000.

David. *Gospel of Matthew: A Homiletical Commentary.* 1873. Reprint, Grand Rapids, MI: Kregel Publications, 1979.

s, Robert L. and Stanley N. Gundry. *A Harmony of the Gospels, with Explanations and Essays.* 1978. Reprint, Chicago, IL: Moody Press, 1981.

ssaint, Stanley D. *Behold the King: A Study of Matthew.* Grand Rapids, MI: Kregel Publications, 1980.

Wallace, Daniel B. *Greek Grammar Beyond the Basics: An Exegetical Syntax of the New Testament.* Grand Rapids, MI: Zondervan, 1996.

Walvoord, John F. *Matthew, Thy Kingdom Come: A Commentary on the First Gospel.* Grand Rapids, MI: Kregel Publications, 1974.

Zodhiates, Spiros. *Exegetical Commentary on Matthew.* Chatanooga, TN: AMG Publishers, 2006.